Space Shuttle

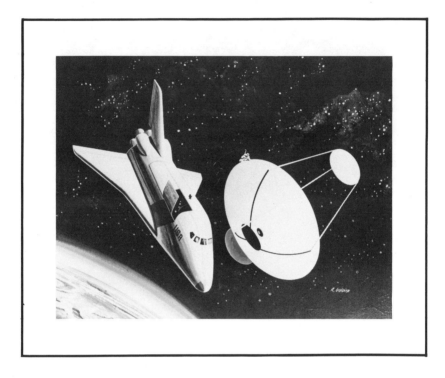

The bowl-shaped antenna of a small space SETI (Search for Extraterrestrial Intelligence) system is carried into low earth orbit and erected in a single flight by the shuttle orbiter.

Space Shuttle

L. B. TAYLOR, JR.

Illustrated with photographs

Thomas Y. Crowell • New York

ALSO BY THE AUTHOR

Gifts from Space:
How Space Technology Is Improving Life on Earth

All photographs courtesy of the National Aeronautics and Space Administration with the exception of page 68 (U.S. Air Force) and page 70 (U.S. Navy).

LIBRARY OF CONGRESS CATALOGING IN PUBLICATION DATA
Taylor, L. B.   Space shuttle.
SUMMARY: Describes the reasons for and the design and operation of NASA's Space Shuttle and discusses who will be flying it and the benefits to be derived from such a shuttle. Bibliography: p.   Includes index. 1. Reusable space vehicles—Juvenile literature. [1. Reusable space vehicles.

2. Space vehicles. 3. Space stations] I. Title   TL795.5.T39   629.45'4   78–4777
ISBN 0–690–03897–6

FIRST EDITION

This book is for Dave Billings,
a very special father-in-law and friend.

ACKNOWLEDGMENTS

Special thanks for provision of background research materials and information is accorded to NASA's Public Information Offices at the Johnson Space Center in Texas, the Kennedy Space Center in Florida, and NASA Headquarters in Washington. I am particularly indebted to Dave Garrett for reviewing the manuscript for factual accuracy, and to my good friends Chuck Hollinshead for his advice and counsel and Margaret Ware for her cheerful assistance in helping provide the photographs for this book.

Contents

1

Commuter Flight to Orbit

At five A.M., an hour before dawn, there is an eerie calm at the John F. Kennedy Space Center, located halfway down the east coast of Florida. Aside from the faraway hum of dozens of generators, a seeming silence masks the furious behind-the-scenes activities of an army of engineers, technicians, equipment operators, and aerospace mechanics.

The velvet blackness is starkly pierced by a battalion of powerful searchlights directing millions of candlepower onto what appears to be an unreal scene. Basking in the brilliant glow on launch pad 39—the same one used in the Apollo moon flights— is a huge cylindrical, 154-foot-long tank, 28.6 feet in diameter, flanked by two rockets, each 150 feet long but half its size in diameter. And mounted in piggy-back fashion on the tank, facing skyward, is what looks like a large jet liner, about the size of a DC-9 aircraft. The entire configuration, painted white, sharply reflects the searchlight beams, giving off a ghostlike appearance for miles in all directions.

This is the space shuttle Enterprise in the final few hours of countdown for a launch into orbit more than a hundred miles above earth.

"T-minus four hours and counting," a spokesman for the National Aeronautics and Space Administration (NASA) announces over a loud-speaker system.

Three miles from the launch pad, more than thirty-five hundred newspaper, magazine, radio and television reporters, photographers, cameramen, and technicians—from the United States and more than seventy nations—have assembled to report this historic event live.

Several more miles away, on the closely guarded third floor of the Operations and Checkout Building, the three astronauts and four passengers—an engineer and three scientists including one woman who will fly aboard Enterprise—are awakened in their sleeping quarters. They arise, shower, and breakfast on orange juice and steak and eggs, a traditional meal dating back to the earliest American manned space flights of Alan Shepard and Gus Grissom in 1961.

"T-minus three hours and counting."

The astronauts and passengers travel by van to the launch pad and ride an elevator up to the cabin of the shuttle orbiter. They enter the craft and are strapped into specially contoured seats 275 feet above the ground. The astronauts begin running down a long checklist involving the forest of gauges and dials before them. They begin with the guidance-alignment checks.

The next 180 minutes pass swiftly, as a thousand details are attended to. The commands ring out from the Launch Control Center, two and a half miles west of the pad.

"Command carrier on."

"Attitude command test complete."

"Power transfer test complete."

"Orbiter on internal power."

In the final minutes the tempo and the tension increase dramatically.

The launch test supervisor asks for final status reports:

"Shuttle test conductor."

"Go."

"Launch operations director."

"Go."

"Launch director."

"Go."

Then the test supervisor says the magic words: "Cleared for launch."

"Firing command on."

The automatic sequencing system is initiated. Computers take over for the final two minutes of the countdown. Propellant tank vents are closed. In the shuttle cockpit, the astronauts visually sweep their instrument panels. All indicators are green.

At T-minus 15 seconds, a thousand motorized cameras on the ground, recording the launch, are set in motion.

"T-minus ten seconds and counting."

Hundreds of thousands of people at the Center and on nearby beaches and causeways squint into the bright Florida sun, many focusing high-powered binoculars, waiting for the instant of launch. Around the world tens of millions of others watch on live television.

"Nine . . . eight . . ."

As the seconds tick down toward zero, the three liquid-fueled main engines on the shuttle orbiter suddenly roar into life. Torrents of blinding, peach-colored flame funnel down onto the asbestos-coated launch pad. An instant later sound catches up to fury as a steady, rolling shock wave of thunder booms across the flatlands, sending hundreds of birds winging.

"Seven . . . six . . . five . . . four . . ."

The seconds now seem longer, stretched out, as the orbiter launch vehicle appears to strain mightily to break the bonds of the tower's hold-down arms. The arms remain clamped for these final few seconds to make sure the booster tank's propellants are burning evenly.

"Three . . . two . . . one . . . zero . . ."

On the precise count of zero the twin rockets ignite in tandem, the hold-down arms retract, and the entire vehicle erupts off the pad like a giant Roman candle.

"Lift-off . . . we have lift-off at 9:04 A.M."

Unlike the Saturn V moon-rocket launches in the late 1960s and early 1970s, which rose with agonizing slowness, because they were entirely liquid fueled, the seven-million-pound shuttle vehicle ascends much faster. This is because its strap-on rockets use solid rather than liquid propellants and burn much faster. They obtain full thrust power in a mere .04 of a second.

In less than half a minute the shuttle clears its launch tower, arcs slight southeast over the Atlantic Ocean, and disappears into a cloudless sky, trailing a thousand-foot, incandescent tail of fire and plumes of white exhaust for miles.

Enterprise is on its way, hurtling toward space like a bullet shot from a rifle. Inside the crew's cabin, the six men and one woman are pushed downward in their seats under pressure one and a half

The space-shuttle orbiter lifts off the launch pad at Kennedy Space Center in Florida. The orbiter's three liquid-fuel rocket engines and two solid-fuel rocket boosters combine to generate more than 6.5 million pounds of thrust. They will obtain full thrust power in .04 of a second.

times greater than the force of gravity. But this is only a momentary sensation and causes no problems.

After two minutes of flight, when the shuttle is 27 miles up and 100 miles down range from the launch pad, the two booster rockets, their job done, burn out. Tiny explosive devices separate them from the shuttle and its external tank, and the two rockets fall back toward the sea. Parachutes deploy, slowing their descent, and a recovery ship moves swiftly toward where they will splash down. They will be towed back to shore for refurbishment and reuse.

The orbiter's three main engines burn for another six minutes, pushing Enterprise to the rim of space. Then they shut down, and the huge cylindrical tank, now empty of propellant, is jettisoned. It tumbles in a 10,000-mile looping arc toward the Indian Ocean. Two small orbital maneuvering engines nudge the shuttle finally up to orbiting speed.

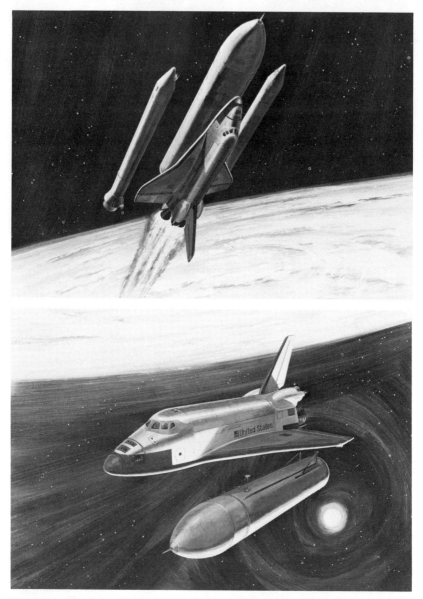

Twenty-seven miles up and two minutes later *(top),* the two booster rockets burn out. Tiny explosive devices separate them from the orbiter and external tank. They fall to a preselected point in the ocean, to be recovered and reused.

After another six minutes *(bottom),* the external tank, emptied of its liquid propellant, separates from the orbiter. Unlike the booster rockets, the external tank is not recoverable. It will break up and disintegrate in the atmosphere over the ocean.

Mission Control at the Lyndon B. Johnson Space Center near Houston, Texas, confirms to an anxious world that the Enterprise has reached orbit. There is a loud cheer of approval from the launch team in the Control Center miles to the east at the Kennedy Space Center. Inside the orbiter, the astronauts and passengers exchange smiles and the thumbs-up sign of initial success.

With short bursts of the small thruster orbital maneuvering engines, the astronauts are able to jockey their large craft into the exact earth-circling groove programmed in the mission's flight plan.

For the next seven days, Enterprise will be home for the astronauts and passengers. It will also be office, workshop, and cafeteria. But unlike the cramped confines of the Apollo spacecraft, which made the round-trip to the moon in eight days, Enterprise is cavernous by comparison, and comfortable.

The first-class accommodations include sleeping quarters, kitchen, bathroom, and work areas. Also, unlike Apollo, in which the astronauts were stuffed cocoonlike into bulky space suits for much of the flight, crew and passengers can perform their tasks in shirt-sleeve ease. The comfort level is much the same as that enjoyed by commercial-airline passengers.

The one big difference, of course, is that those aboard Enterprise are weightless when in orbit. Space is a vacuum; there is no gravity. So to keep from floating about, everyone must either be strapped down or hold on to something. Movement is easy. If you wish to go one way, you merely push the other way, thus exercising Newton's third law: For every action there is an equal and opposite reaction.

Behind the living area is the orbiter's immense cargo bay, capable of holding more than 32 tons of payload, or cargo. On this particular mission a new weather satellite is housed in the bay. After it has been checked out by the mission specialist and the meteorologist aboard, spindly, robotlike arms deploy it in orbit from the opened doors of the cargo bay. It will serve on station for years, observing, recording, and reporting earth's weather as it develops, and relaying information instantly to ground stations at strategic points around the world.

Meanwhile, the other two scientists are occupied with their individual projects. The woman, an astronomer, is to make a special study of flares on the sun's surface. She uses a large, powerful telescope, and because she can observe the solar disk without the ever-shimmering veil of atmospheric haze that blankets the earth, she is able to see her subject with a clarity impossible to gain on earth.

The other scientist is an expert in geology. He is observing and monitoring fault systems in the earth, gathering data that may lead to accurate predictions of the time, location, and intensity of earthquakes.

This cutaway view shows the crew at their duty stations in the orbiter's flight deck. Behind the flight deck the payload bay doors have just opened to release a payload into earth orbit. Some of the forward compartment area can be seen below the flight deck.

The astronauts, too, are busy during the week in orbit. In addition to keeping check on the computers that control Enterprise's precise orbital maneuvers, they take turns photographing the rotating earth below. They also conduct exercise sessions for the group and use sophisticated medical equipment constantly to assess everyone's health. Throughout the mission this information is instantaneously relayed to doctors at the Houston Control Center.

Meals are enjoyed. For one thing, the food is considerably better than the bite-size, dehydrated food eaten during the early space flights. The conversations are lively as everyone shares their experiences of the day. There is little leisure time, for there is much work to do, but a highlight is looking out of Enterprise's windows to see sunrise and sunset rushing past at a phenomenal rate of speed, as the shuttle completely circles the earth once every ninety minutes.

Still, strangely, there is absolutely no sensation of speed inside the craft. Sleep the first night or two does not come easily for the passengers. Used to lying horizontally on a bed, they find it odd that in the weightless environment, standing up is the same as lying down.

All too soon, seven days have passed, and Enterprise must head for home. The orbiter is turned around, so that its orbital engines face the direction of travel. A short burn of the engines slows the shuttle's speed, gradually dropping it nearer the earth's atmosphere.

The astronauts now turn the craft around again and point the nose up at a sharp 40-degree angle. Computers take over. At the upper reaches of earth's gravitational pull, 400,000 feet over Hawaii, a slight vibration is felt inside. As the shuttle rapidly descends, surface temperatures soar to a fiery 2,700 degrees Fahrenheit, but the underside of the vehicle has a shield specially built to withstand the heat; inside the cabin the temperature remains normal.

Eight minutes into reentry, the shuttle's nose drops down, and it becomes, in effect, a giant glider, steering a zigzag pattern to reduce its still tremendous speed of more than 180 miles a minute. The southern part of the United States from California to Texas flashes by below. Then the Gulf of Mexico is swiftly crossed.

Over Orlando, Florida, in the middle of the state, the shuttle has slowed to twice the speed of sound, and dropped to an altitude of 20,000 feet. The orbiter banks to the east, aligning itself for final approach to landing at a three-mile-long concrete apron adjoining the Kennedy Space Center. The landing area is only a few miles from the launching pad where the journey began a week ago.

On-board computers smartly respond to the Center's automated landing system. Enterprise hits a steep 24-degree angle, then at 1,700 feet begins to level off a mile and a half from the edge of the runway at a landing speed of more than 200 miles per hour. Seconds later, landing gear in place, the hulking vehicle touches down, much like a 747 jet aircraft, and brakes to a smooth stop.

The mission is completed.

The three astronauts, after cleaning up, are debriefed by officials. The scientists and the engineer begin the long months of work, reporting and analyzing the results of their projects. And the Enterprise is taken to the Vehicle Assembly Building nearby, where it will be readied for another flight to space—possibly within a few weeks.

Mission completed, the orbiter returns to Kennedy Space Center. The orbiter will be able to land on a conventional runway similar to those used by present-day jet aircraft.

2

Why the Shuttle?

Such a mission as flown by Enterprise is not a fantasy. Shuttle flights to and from earth orbit will be commonplace events in the 1980s—and they will change our lives.

Just what is this ungainly-looking new space system and how did it come into being? What will happen to the sleek rockets that for years launched men to the moon and unmanned spacecraft to the far reaches of our solar system? What does it mean when NASA that says the shuttle is to usher in Phase II of the nation's space program?

The origins of the shuttle program began in the late 1960s. But the early planning was all but lost in the overwhelming amount of attention focused on the initial manned lunar landing in July

1969. It was an exciting time, and few people then looked beyond those historic first steps taken on the moon's surface by astronauts Neil Armstrong and Buzz Aldrin.

Still, the long-range planners in NASA and those in the American spacecraft industry knew that once the moon had been explored, it would signal the beginning of the end for one era of the space program—and it would also mark the dawning of another.

Phase I was the exploration of space. For the first dozen years, after the opening of the Space Age in October 1957 with the launching of the tiny Russian satellite, Sputnik I, every effort was concentrated on mastering the sheer engineering feat of getting to and from space safely.

This, of course, was a vast undertaking that involved hundreds of thousands of scientists, engineers, technicians, skilled craftsmen, and others. Working together as never before, they forged scores of magnificent technological breakthroughs as they reached farther upward and outward into the unknown.

Thousands of difficult technical questions had to be answered. How to escape earth's bonds of gravity? How to place satellites into orbit above earth? How to launch a spacecraft toward a steadily moving target, such as the moon or a planet, so that perhaps millions of miles from earth both the craft and the target would reach the same place at the same time? How to build a heat shield for returning spacecraft that would withstand torrid reentry into the earth's atmosphere, where temperatures might sizzle to 5,000 degrees Fahrenheit? Would human beings be able to survive in space? Would they be able to work effectively? What would their reaction be to the gravity-free environment of space? These are just a representative few of the complex problems that had to be solved.

Thus, it is little wonder that the landing on the moon has been called the greatest single engineering achievement in the history of civilization.

It was also one of the most expensive. It is estimated that the Apollo moon-landing program alone cost approximately $25 billion. So after several other successful manned flights to the lunar surface in the early 1970s, the luster of excitement and the thrill of discovery and exploration began to dull.

The American public, which essentially funds the space program through the payment of federal taxes, began to ask some serious questions. With so many problems at home—such as poverty, hunger, the energy shortage, and environmental pollution—why continue the exploration of space? After all, we had proved we could do it. How was the conquest of space going to better our lives on earth?

The answers to these questions led to changing the entire emphasis of the space program, to redirecting the primary thrust from the exploration of space to the development of its uses. It was time to begin considering the limitless potential of space to improve things on earth.

Even in the early 1970s, many such applications were already becoming evident. Weather satellites were giving us early warnings of approaching hurricanes, and therefore saving the agricultural, shipping, and construction industries, among others, billions of dollars a year with faster and more accurate weather forecasts. Other satellites were relaying telephone, telegraph, and television communications to the distant corners of the world with unprecedented speed. Astronauts had proved that from orbit we could better survey and manage this planet's resources. And literally thousands of "spin-off" benefits from space technology in such areas as air and highway safety, fireproof clothing, medical innovations, energy-saving ideas, and improved household items, ranging from digital clocks to freeze-dried foods and liquids, were being adapted for use on earth.

Still, the price of these benefits was far too high. Each rocket launched at the Kennedy Space Center cost millions of dollars. The rocket engines alone cost millions. Yet, once they burned out, shoving their assorted payloads toward space, the rockets fell back into the ocean and were lost in a watery grave, never to be used again. Each individual spacecraft, too, took much money, labor, and time to build and assemble. Yet one tiny part that malfunctioned in space might render the whole craft useless. Even satellites that worked well would eventually run out of power, only to continue orbiting earth as mute pieces of metallic junk.

Clearly an entirely new and less expensive means of space transportation must be developed. Dr. Kurt H. Debus, former director of the Kennedy Space Center, summed up the problem: "Business," he said, "does not discard a Greyhound bus after its first trip from New York to Miami. But that, in effect, is what NASA and the Department of Defense must do every time a space mission is launched with conventional rockets."

In a nutshell, the key to the problem was to design a reusable system; rocket and spacecraft hardware that could be launched into space, perform missions in orbit, and then return to earth to be overhauled and used again—the more often, the better.

With this idea in mind, NASA and a special Space Task Group assigned by the President of the United States began serious studies to provide such a system. The group suggested that the United States develop a space transportation system that would "carry passengers, supplies, rocket fuel, other spacecraft, equipment, or additional rocket stages to and from orbit on a routine, aircraft-like basis."

Endorsing the recommendation of the group, President Richard M. Nixon, on January 5, 1972, said:

... the United States should proceed at once with the development of an entirely new type of space transportation system designed to help transform the space frontier of the 1970s into familiar territory, easily accessible for human endeavor in the 1980s and 1990s.

This system will center on a space vehicle that can shuttle repeatedly from earth to orbit and back . . . it will go a long way toward delivering the rich benefits of practical space use and the valuable spinoffs from space efforts into the daily lives of Americans and all people.

. . . the space shuttle program is the right next step for America to take, in moving out from our present beachhead in the sky to achieve a real working presence in space. [The shuttle] will make the ride safer and less demanding for the passengers, so that men and women with work to do in space can commute aloft, without having to spend years in training.

"We must sail sometimes with the wind and sometimes against it," said Oliver Wendell Holmes, "but we must sail, and not drift, nor lie at anchor." So [it is] with man's epic voyage into space— a voyage the United States of America has led and still shall lead.

With that presidential proclamation, issued during the first week of 1972, the space shuttle officially was born, and with it, a new era of space flight that will affect our lives for the rest of this century and perhaps beyond.

3

The Lessons of Skylab

Before the use of space for the benefit of mankind could be fully developed, and before the United States federal government could justify investing billions of dollars into an orbital transportation system, it had to be proven conclusively that man could safely and comfortably live and work in orbit for relatively long periods of time.

From the earliest days of the Russian and American space flights, it was known that man could survive in this new weightless environment above earth. Dozens of cosmonauts and astronauts verified that fact throughout the 1960s. But the majority of these missions lasted for only several hours, or a few days at most. And in the cramped quarters of Mercury, Gemini, Apollo, and Soyuz spacecraft, the crews were restricted in what they could do. They were little more than space pilots most of the time.

With the shuttle flights calling for periods of orbit ranging from a week to a month, more data on the long-term effects of space on humans had to be obtained. Hundreds of questions had to be answered.

The answers came through a NASA program called Skylab. The idea for Skylab was simple. NASA would launch a temporary space station into earth orbit. Actually, it would be a refurbished third stage of the Saturn V moon rocket: a huge cylindrical shell 48 feet long and 21 feet in diameter, encompassing about 10,000 cubic feet of space.

The engines of this silolike stage of the rocket would be removed, and all the complex plumbing it normally carried would be stripped out. Skylab would be refitted to serve as a home away from home for a team of three astronauts for periods ranging from one to two months or longer.

Grid-pattern floors and ceilings were installed in the tank, separating living and laboratory working areas into a two-story arrangement. In the tail end of the cylinder, solid partitions were designed to divide the crew's living quarters into separate sleeping compartments, a dining area, a bathroom, and a working, or office section. The other end of Skylab, covering about three quarters of the total space, was outfitted as a giant laboratory where most of the experimental work was to be done.

Three separate teams of astronauts lived and worked in Skylab at different times. Each was launched from earth in a modified Apollo spacecraft, similar to the ones that carried astronauts to the moon. The craft would dock with the Skylab complex about 230 miles up in earth orbit. The crew would enter and leave the huge tank through an air-lock module. And they would return to earth in the Apollo in the same way as all previous manned space flights—by reentering earth's atmosphere and splashing down in the ocean.

The first crew was to open up the workshop area of Skylab and stay in orbit for about a month. Then they would close up their "house" and return to earth. After an interval the second crew would go up and return, and then the third one, each team in turn staying in orbit for a longer period.

It did not take long for the astronauts to prove the value of human ingenuity in space. About a minute after the Skylab tank was launched, on May 14, 1973, an aluminum micrometeoroid shield ripped away. Skylab continued into orbit, but within an hour after lift-off, ground controllers on earth realized the flight was in trouble. They had received no radioed signals from space indicating that the two largest solar panels had opened on each side of the workshop. The mechanism that should have unlocked them must somehow have malfunctioned; perhaps it had been damaged when the shielding tore away.

The problem was critical. Without the use of these two panels, which converted sunlight to electricity, Skylab's electrical capacity would be cut in half. Many of the key experiments planned would have to be scrapped. Then further trouble developed.

Skylab's unprotected metal hull heated up to nearly 300 degrees Fahrenheit during its first day in orbit, and the interior of the tank, where the astronauts were to live, became like an oven. Temperatures inside averaged 120 degrees. Obviously the astronauts could not operate under these conditions, so their launch to dock with Skylab was postponed. Officials feared that the intense heat would spoil food and damage medicines and photographic film aboard the orbiting vehicle. Some feared that

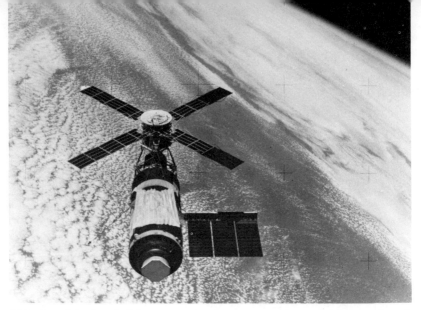

This view of the first Skylab space-station cluster, seen against a cloud-covered earth, was photographed from the Skylab 3 Command and Service Module. A makeshift sunshade was installed to replace a solar shield lost on launch day. The solar panel on the left-hand side was also lost.

the whole $2.5 billion Skylab program would be lost before it had scarcely begun.

But the space engineers on earth went to work. They quickly designed an aluminized awning of Mylar, an extremely thin mirrorlike plastic foil, for the astronauts to erect in space. This would shade Skylab enough to protect it from the heat of the sun, thus lowering the temperatures inside the workshop to acceptable levels.

Still, only the three astronauts themselves, 230 miles above earth, could erect the new shield. The team of Charles Conrad, Paul Weitz, and Joseph Kerwin was launched on May 25—ten days late. The following day they were able to open successfully their makeshift sunshade, and the temperature inside the workshop began to drop to livable levels. A few days later Conrad and Kerwin, standing outside Skylab with their bodies extended in space, snapped loose a jammed bolt, and the solar panel sprouted out and open. This would provide the additional electric power needed throughout the three-flight Skylab mission.

By successfully accomplishing these two tricky repair jobs in earth orbit, Conrad, Weitz, and Kerwin demonstrated man's ability to improvise and work effectively in a weightless environment, solving technical problems that might otherwise have caused cancellation of the entire program.

The first team of astronauts stayed in space for twenty-eight days, far longer than anyone ever had before. And they completed a tremendous amount of work. With a special telescope mount, they took more than thirty thousand pictures of regions of the sun for scientists to study. They also took photo images of 182 sites in thirty-one states and nine foreign nations. Such data would be used to assemble weather and pollution-pattern information—to aid geologists and oceanographers and land-use managers, among others, by providing overviews of earth from an orbital vantage.

During the four-week-long flight, astronaut Kerwin, a doctor, conducted extensive medical tests, and found that he himself and his two fellow crew members remained in excellent health. "This gives us tremendous encouragement about future long-duration flights," he commented.

A month and a half after the end of the first Skylab flight, on July 28, 1973, the second team of astronauts was launched. Alan Bean, Jack Lousma, and Owen Garriott stayed in space more than twice as long as the first crew—59 days. Again volumes of useful scientific and medical data were assembled.

More than 77,000 pictures of the sun and 14,000 pictures of the earth were taken. Space cameras tracked tropical storms and locust swarms and surveyed crop growth and water resources in many parts of the world. Snowfields in the Swiss Alps, geologi-

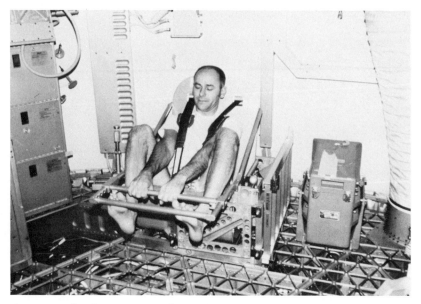

Astronaut Alan Bean, commander of the Skylab 2 crew, conducts a body-mass measurement experiment in the orbital workshop.

Dr. Owen Garriott, science pilot of the Skylab 2 crew, reconstitutes food in the orbital workshop.

Astronaut William Pogue, pilot of the Skylab 3 crew, holds on to the ceiling of the orbital workshop crew quarters as he prepares to jump onto the airlock hatch cover to force a trash bag down into the airlock. Astronaut Gerald Carr, commander, holding on to two more trash bags, assists him. Another trash bag floats near Pogue's leg in the zero-gravity environment.

Standing at the Apollo Telescope Mount console in the airlock module of the Skylab space-station cluster is Astronaut Edward Gibson, Skylab 3 science pilot. The console controls several instruments on the solar telescope, mounted outside.

cally interesting features in space, and industrial pollution in Germany were all captured on film. Further vital data was gathered during Skylab passes over the United States, South and Central America, and Asia.

In one experiment of special interest, astronaut Lousma fired up an electrical furnace taken into space to form new metal alloys that will not blend on earth because of gravity. The results of this test provided exciting new information about the action of materials in a weightless environment which could be used in planning for future manufacturing in space on a large scale.

Despite the fact that this second team of astronauts "traveled" more than 24 million miles around earth during their nearly two-month stay in orbit, doctors were extremely pleased by the astronauts' excellent physical condition when they returned home.

The final Skylab flight, with astronauts Gerald Carr, Edward Gibson, and William Pogue aboard, began November 16, 1973, and ran for a record-setting 84 days. This crew concentrated on collecting data on seasonal changes, the development of sea and lake ice, snow-cover patterns, major storms, and changes in vegetation in the northern and southern hemispheres.

They brought back enough photographs, magnetic tapes, and other data to keep researchers and scientists busy for years. And they, too, came back in good health, with no apparent lasting ill effects from their long stay in space. In all, hundreds of experiments were successfully accomplished during the three missions.

Skylab thus proved without question that human beings could adapt to live and work safely, comfortably, and effectively in zero-gravity conditions for relatively long periods of time. This was the exact type of information needed to go ahead confidently with the development of the space shuttle.

4

Designing a Space Truck

Aerospace engineers had to go back to the drawing boards to design and build the space-shuttle transportation system. Individual components of the system were not new. The orbiter would be launched into space by conventional rockets. In orbit, it would function as a spacecraft. And upon its return to earth, it would fly much like an airplane.

But the trick was to combine all these features—rocket, spacecraft, and airplane—into one vehicle. That was something that had never yet been done.

And there were design complexities. To fulfill the promise of economy through reusability, the major units of the system would have to be devised so that they could withstand the physical punishment of space flight, be retrieved, and then be refurbished for further missions. The orbiter and its booster system would have to be durable.

During its reentry into the earth's atmosphere down through landing on the ground, the shuttle orbiter would be flying through three separate flight ranges: hypersonic (five or more times the speed of sound); supersonic (one to five times the speed of sound); and subsonic (below the speed of sound). So the vehicle would have to be flexible in design. The flights themselves would have to be made more comfortable than any in the past, because nonastronauts would be aboard. Acceleration and deceleration forces during ascent and reentry would have to be lessened.

To draw the blueprints and build the hardware, NASA sought help from some of the nation's leading aerospace companies. Thousands of aerodynamics experts began brainstorming, matching capabilities of literally hundreds of designs to the strict shuttle-flight requirements.

Slowly the outlines of the new vehicle began to emerge. To cut costs, officials agreed on using a conventional rocket system to propel the orbiter into space, rather than building boosters that would return to earth with the orbiter. This way, the rockets could be fished out of the sea after their job was done, returned to the launch site, and be readied for another flight.

An early straight-wing orbiter configuration was replaced with a delta, or triangular-wing concept to give the vehicle more flight maneuverability during its return from space to earth. As these and other design changes evolved, NASA in July 1972 selected a prime contractor to build the shuttle: Rockwell International, the company that had previously developed the Apollo moon command and service modules, various rocket stages, and most of the nation's space-boosting engines.

For the next few years, Rockwell and hundreds of important subcontractors throughout the United States began the long complex process of transforming the shuttle system from paper to reality.

A cutaway view of the complete space-shuttle system. The airplane-like orbiter sits atop the large external propellant tank, which fuels the orbiter's three liquid hydrogen/liquid oxygen main engines. Twin solid-rocket boosters flank the propellant tank.

Following is a summary description of the shuttle's key components:

• The orbiter itself looks like a misshapen jet liner. It has a fat fuselage, stubby wings, and huge engines mounted at its aft end. Without fuel, it weighs approximately 150,000 pounds and is 122 feet long. Its wingspan is only 78 feet.

Dominating the orbiter design is its vast cargo bay, which measures 60 feet in length. In this cavernous compartment, payloads up to 65,000 pounds can be carried to orbit. A long, spindly manipulator arm, operated by remote control, will be used to place satellites and experiments into space, and to retrieve other spacecraft when the cargo bay's doors are open.

The three-story cabin is designed as a combination working and living area. The upper section, or flight deck, contains the displays and controls used by astronauts to pilot, monitor, and control the vehicle in flight and to work the mission payloads. Seating for up to four crew members is provided in much the same manner as on a jet liner, with pilot and copilot sitting side by side, mission specialist and payload expert seated behind.

The midsection includes passenger seating, the living area, with working, sleeping, dining, and bathroom facilities, and compartments for electronic equipment. Every cubic inch of space has been designed for maximum use. While the living area is not spacious—it is roughly equivalent in size to one fourth the area of a small three-bedroom house—there is enough room for ten people in all, although on most missions no more than seven will fly. They will be comfortable, breathing 20 percent oxygen and 80 percent nitrogen at a pressure of 14.7 pounds per square inch —conditions just like those enjoyed on earth at sea level.

The space-shuttle orbiter

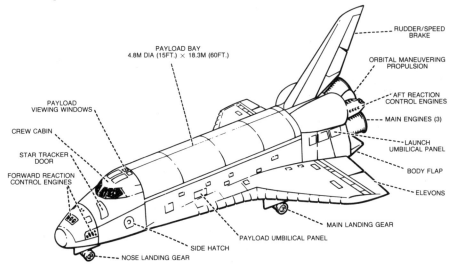

RUDDER/SPEED BRAKE

ORBITAL MANEUVERING PROPULSION

PAYLOAD BAY
4.8M DIA (15FT.) × 18.3M (60FT.)

AFT REACTION CONTROL ENGINES

MAIN ENGINES (3)

PAYLOAD VIEWING WINDOWS

LAUNCH UMBILICAL PANEL

CREW CABIN

STAR TRACKER DOOR

BODY FLAP

FORWARD REACTION CONTROL ENGINES

ELEVONS

MAIN LANDING GEAR

PAYLOAD UMBILICAL PANEL

SIDE HATCH

NOSE LANDING GEAR

Orbiter cabin

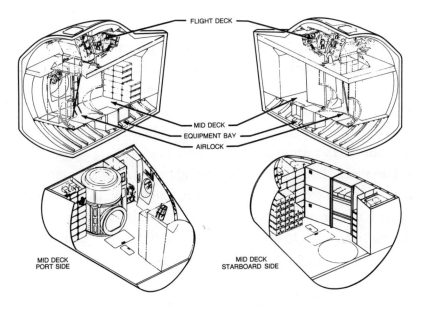

FLIGHT DECK

MID DECK
EQUIPMENT BAY
AIRLOCK

MID DECK
PORT SIDE

MID DECK
STARBOARD SIDE

The lower section of the cabin is used to store environmental-control equipment. Just behind the cabin is an air lock, through which crew members may exit for extravehicular activity, or "walks" in space.

The orbiter has two main power systems, one to supply electrical power and another for hydraulic power. Much of the electrical system is to be used for payload handling and operations. Three independent hydraulic fluid systems will provide the power for flight, including operation of elevons, rudder, body flap, main engine maneuvering, control systems, landing-gear brakes, and steering.

The orbiter's avionics package includes communications and tracking systems; guidance, navigation, and control systems; flight displays, controls, and instruments; and five on-board digital computers for data processing.

A separate environmental-control system regulates cabin atmosphere (temperature, pressure, humidity, carbon-dioxide level, and odor). Precise environmental control is vital not only to sustain life aboard the orbiter, but also to keep delicate instruments and experiments in top working order.

Overall, the orbiter structure is built primarily of aluminum protected by reusable surface insulation. Portions of the outer surface of the vehicle, especially the underside, are covered with thermal materials to protect orbiter from the excessive heat—up to 3,000 degrees Fahrenheit—it will experience during its reentry into the earth's atmosphere.

• The space shuttle's large cylindrical external tank—more than half the distance of a football field in length and over 28 feet in diameter—carries the propellants for the orbiter's main engines during the launch-to-orbit phase of each flight. The same type of fuel—liquid oxygen and liquid nitrogen—as was used to boost

The external tank for the space shuttle is rolled out at the Michoud Assembly Facility near New Orleans, Louisiana, September 9, 1977. It will hold liquid fuel for the three engines on the space-shuttle orbiter.

moon-bound astronauts toward space will be used. At lift-off, the filled tank will contain more than one and a half million pounds of propellants.

• The twin solid-fuel rocket boosters, strapped to the sides of the external tank, will burn for about two minutes in concert with the orbiter's main engines, to provide the initial thrust necessary to propel the shuttle through earth's gravitational bonds toward space. Each booster is about 150 feet long and weighs nearly 1.3 million pounds before launch.

• On the orbiter vehicle itself are the three main propulsion engines. Each is about 14 feet long with a nozzle almost 8 feet in diameter. Fuel will be pumped to the engines through piping connected to the external tank.

An orbital maneuvering subsystem and the orbiter's reaction-control subsystem each use smaller engines and thrusters to insert the shuttle into orbit, maneuver and control it for speed changes and transfers from one orbit to another, and jockey it into position for reentry into earth's atmosphere.

These are the primary components of the space shuttle. Construction of the first vehicle, designated Orbiter 101, without the booster rockets or external tank, was begun in mid-1974. Rockwell International, as prime contractor to NASA, was responsible for the final assembly, and also built the crew module and the aft section of the fuselage at the company's Space Division in Downey, California.

The space-shuttle orbiter is being hoisted to a mating position with the external tank and solid-rocket boosters in the Vehicle Assembly Building at the Kennedy Space Center, Florida. When operational, the space shuttle can be launched on a new mission about two weeks after the orbiter has landed from the preceding mission.

Enterprise Orbiter 101 on the day of its rollout for its first public viewing, shown here at the Rockwell International Space Division orbiter-assembly facility at Palmdale, California. The four astronauts chosen for the Space Shuttle Approach and Landing Test are *(left to right)* Gordon Fullerton, Fred Haise, Joe Engle, and Richard Truly.

Meanwhile other main parts came from numerous aerospace contractors throughout the nation. The mid-fuselage section, including the cargo-bay area, was built by General Dynamics in San Diego, California; wings were constructed by Grumman Aerospace Corporation in Bethpage, New York; and the tail assembly was fashioned by Fairchild Republic Company, Farmingdale, New York. The orbiter's three main engines were manufactured by Rockwell's Rocketdyne Division in Canoga Park, California. Each of these main contractors was, in turn, supported and supplied by nearly 10,000 subcontractors and small companies.

Final assembly and mating began in August 1975, and a little more than a year later, on September 17, 1976, Orbiter 101 was rolled out for its first public display. Late in January 1977, the vehicle was transported by truck thirty-five miles north to NASA's Dryden Flight Research Center at Edwards, California.

On February 15, 1977, mounted piggyback atop a 747 jet aircraft, 101 performed a series of taxi tests to gather data on ground handling and control of this enormous (544,000 pounds) and unseemly-looking flight combination.

Three days later, the 747, again carrying Orbiter 101 on its back, took off for a two-hour test flight. Results were far better than officials had expected. In fact, the 747 crew stated they "couldn't even tell the orbiter was aboard." Actually, with the orbiter, the 747 jet still weighed less than it did when fully loaded with passengers, baggage, and enough fuel for a transcontinental flight.

Test flights continued through most of the year. The first five were targeted at checking out the aerodynamic design of the orbiter. A second series of tests, with two astronauts at the controls of 101, was conducted with all systems aboard the orbiter activated.

Next came the first of a series of "free flights," where after all systems had been checked out in the air, the orbiter would be separated from its 747 mother ship to glide in for a landing on its own.

There was considerable nervousness at the Dryden Research Center on the morning of August 12, 1977, when this first test was scheduled. Even though everything humanly possible had been done to assure a successful mission, it still was the first time the orbiter had been on its own. The design on paper was fine.

The space-shuttle Enterprise orbiter aboard the 747 carrier *(top)* takes off on the first manned captive flight on June 18, 1977. Flutter checks, the orbiter speed brake, and control stick steering were checked out during the initial manned captive test. The flight lasted 55 minutes. In a test series of "free flights" *(middle)* the orbiter separates from its 747 mother ship, is piloted through a series of maneuvers, and *(bottom)* glides in for a landing of its own.

But would it work well in reality? There is always a certain amount of tension during the first flight test of any flying craft.

As the 747 rolled down the long runway for takeoff, astronauts Fred Haise and Gordon Fullerton checked the controls and monitors on the orbiter. Less than an hour after takeoff, the moment of truth came. Explosive bolts were fired, releasing the 101 vehicle from the 747 at an altitude of about four miles. From the orbiter's cockpit, the operation sounded like the muted pop of a champagne cork. There was a moderate jolt forcing the astronauts down in their seats, then silence.

For the next five minutes, Haise and Fullerton piloted the orbiter through a series of maneuvers. Although it had no engines of its own, the astronauts decreased and increased the speed of the orbiter by pitching its nose up and down. Then they made two long 90-degree turns to the left to align the craft with a runway on a dry lake bed below.

As cameras whirred, computers controlled and data recorders collected each minute detail, and anxious ground controllers watched, the orbiter performed perfectly. It touched down a little more than five minutes after separation, at a speed of 207 miles per hour, and braked to a smooth stop. Orbiter 101 had won its wings—at least its wings in earth's atmosphere.

Four more free flights followed in the next two and a half months, and they were all so successful that further test runs were canceled.

The next phase of the program shifted across the country in the spring of 1978, when Orbiter 101 was flown atop the 747 to the Marshall Space Flight Center in Huntsville, Alabama, for vertical ground-vibration tests. Here it was mated with its external tank and strap-on booster rockets and stood on its tail—in the same posture in which it will eventually be launched into space —in a dynamic test facility.

These torture tests, in which the entire orbiter configuration is literally violently shaken, are designed to simulate the vibration and stress loads the vehicle will encounter during its launch phase. At launch, when all the shuttle engines—the three main engines of the orbiter and the two solid boosters—fire simultaneously, 6.8 million pounds of thrust will be generated.

From these important tests, engineers gained information needed for analysis of flight-control stability and dynamic loads that would occur during the launch and flight-to-space phases of the mission. Again 101 passed with high marks.

This concluded the earth-testing part of the shuttle-development program. Next would come the real thing: a series of six manned test flights into orbit and back to earth. These would run into 1980. Once all the test objectives of this series have been met, a new space transportation system will begin regular operations.

5

Anyone – Almost – Can Fly

NASA began looking for astronauts to pilot America's first manned space program, Project Mercury, in the late 1950s. An extremely difficult set of qualification standards was set up. Candidates had to be less than forty years of age; less than 5 feet 11 inches in height; in extraordinarily good physical condition; have a bachelor's degree from an accredited college or university, or its equivalent; be a graduate of a test-pilot school; have a total of at least 1,500 hours of flying time; and be a qualified jet pilot.

This set of standards, of course, automatically eliminated more than 99 percent of the potential applicants, including all women. No women pilots at that time could meet the combined last three qualifications—test-pilot-school graduate; qualified jet pilot with a total of 1,500 hours of flying time. In fact, when these standards were cross-checked with the records of all American pilots then in the military service, only slightly more than a hundred men appeared to meet the initial qualifications.

Excruciatingly tough physical and psychological tests were given to those in this select group who were interested in becoming space pilots. The tests and the screening program to choose the first astronauts lasted for several months, and resulted in the naming of the seven original astronauts.

Their training program was long and grueling. They were strapped into centrifuges and whipped about in circles at great rates of speed to simulate the effects of the high acceleration and deceleration forces they would experience during the launch phase of space flight. They were dropped off in remote mountain and desert regions and left to live off the land for days at a time as a part of survival training. This would prepare them should their spacecraft land unexpectedly in uninhabited or hostile parts of the world upon their return from space. Over all, it was a long, torturous program that only a few people—perhaps one in ten thousand—could first qualify for and then endure.

As the manned-space programs evolved from Mercury to Gemini and then to the Apollo moon-landing missions, NASA had need for additional astronauts, and a few restrictions were eased. The height limitation was raised to 6 feet, for example, but basically the qualifications required continued to limit the number of candidates. This pattern continued into the 1970s through the Skylab series of earth-orbital flights.

The advent of the shuttle program changed all this.

For one thing, a much larger number of crew members will have to be available to draw upon for the flights of the 1980s. In the Mercury, Gemini, Apollo, and Skylab programs, there usually was an interval of several months, sometimes even years, between manned flights. By 1985, however, NASA expects to be launching as many as sixty shuttle missions a year into earth orbit, carrying as many as seven people on some.

A number of these specific flights will be of a highly specialized nature, which, in some cases, will involve months of intense, close-knit training. Individual shuttle teams, then, may well work together for periods up to a year or longer before their particular craft is launched. And with more than a flight a week scheduled by the mid-1980s, the need for a much larger contingent of astronauts and crew members is obvious.

A second major point that has led to the easing of flight qualifications for shuttle candidates is tied to the scientific nature of many of the planned missions. One of the main criticisms of the Apollo moon-landing program was that the astronaut explorers were mostly engineer-oriented and lacked training as scientists. The scientific community said the lunar explorations would have been far more meaningful had they been carried out by geologists or seismic experts or mineralogists.

This was at least partially proved during the final flight of the lunar program, Apollo 17, in December 1972. One of the astronauts on that mission was Dr. Harrison Schmitt, a geologist with a PhD degree from Harvard who had been a Fulbright scholar. Among other things, Schmitt discovered a "bright orange" type of soil in the moon's Taurus Littrow area, which suggested that this region may contain relatively young volcanic features. The material appeared to be a finely structured glass of volcanic origin.

Schmitt's on-the-scene observations and comments throughout Apollo 17's exploratory period greatly aided scientists on earth in their studies, and convincingly demonstrated the great contributions a trained scientist in space can make.

But Schmitt was a rarity: a brilliant scientist who also had considerable advanced flight training. NASA realizes today that it is very difficult, if not impossible, for people to pursue dual careers, both as a jet pilot and as a scientist in a specialized field. So this is another reason for the easing of restrictions for some shuttle crew members.

A third consideration was based on the experience gained in the Skylab series of flights. These missions proved that from a medical standpoint, humans could operate efficiently in space for a relatively long period of time—up to almost three months—without endangering their health. Following his return from the first Skylab mission, astronaut Charles Conrad commented, "I'd say very definitely that the average man or woman could fly in space."

The physical restraints of crew members will be considerably eased during the launch phase of the shuttle in comparison to past rocket flights. The crew will undergo much less acceleration stress. Also, once on station in orbit, they can perform in "shirt-sleeve" comfort.

Even during the times when space suits will be necessary, when working outside the orbiter's pressurized compartments, the task will be far easier. This is because of a new, more flexible space-suit design that can be adjusted to fit both men and women. It comes in two parts—upper torso and pants—and each part is pressure-sealed. The material used for the elbow, knee, and other joints is a fabric that allows freer movement, and the suits themselves both cost and weigh less than earlier ones.

Each shuttle flight will carry both professional pilots of the highest skill and scientists in varying fields of endeavor. Actually,

The new space-shuttle space suit, or extravehicular mobility unit (EMU), is designed to allow space travelers to perform more tasks with much less physical exertion than did the equipment worn by the Apollo astronauts. The new two-piece suit has an upper torso made of rigid aluminum, with the life-support backpack permanently attached. Here, after the space suit is pressurized, the astronaut disconnects the upper torso and backpack from the shuttle bulkhead, and is free to move about.

there will be three types of shuttle crew members: pilots, mission specialists, and payload specialists.

At least two pilots will be on each mission. One of the pilots will serve as commander of the flight. The commander and pilot will be responsible for control of the shuttle during launch, reentry, and all other required maneuvers, and for maintenance of the shuttle system.

The commander will have on-board responsibility for the space vehicle, crew, mission success, and safety of the flight. The pilot will assist the commander in controlling and operating the shuttle. The pilot also may deploy and retrieve payloads using the remote manipulator system. He or she may participate in extravehicular activities, such as space walks, if necessary, and support certain payload operations where appropriate.

Pilot-astronaut candidates must meet the following minimum qualifications:

1. Have a bachelor's degree from an accredited institution in engineering, physical science, or mathematics. An advanced degree (master's or doctorate), or equivalent experience, is desired.

2. Have at least 1,000 hours pilot time, with 2,000 or more being desirable. High-performance jet aircraft and flight test experience is highly desirable.

3. Have the ability to pass a tough flight physical examination.

4. Be between 5 feet 4 inches and 6 feet 4 inches in height. NASA has been able to lift the height limitation of pilot candidates because there will be considerably more room aboard the shuttle than there was in the much smaller Mercury, Gemini, and Apollo spacecraft.

Mission specialists, like the pilot astronauts, will be selected and trained by NASA, but they do not have to meet the same strict flight requirements. One mission specialist will accompany each flight crew, and he or she will have overall responsibility for coordinating operations in areas of crew activity, planning, consumables' usage (such as food, water, fuel, etc.), and other work affecting experiment operations.

Mission specialists will undergo fairly rigorous training because they may be called upon to perform space walks outside the safe confines of the orbiter during missions. Such walks may be necessary to activate or operate equipment or experiments, or to retrieve experimental packages that have been exposed to space. In addition, they will perform special payload-handling assignments, such as maneuvering the shuttle's manipulator arm. And they may be called upon to assist in specific experimental operations at the request of payload sponsors—the people who are paying to have experiments or other cargo flown on the shuttle.

The remainder of the crew will consist of one to four payload specialists who need not have been members of the astronaut training program. Rather, they may be nominated by the sponsor of the specific payload being flown. They will be in charge of the operation of specific payload equipment where their special skills are needed. Such specialists may include geologists, hydrologists, astronomers, meteorologists, communications experts, environmentalists, or others especially qualified in one or more scientific disciplines. Or they may be engineers or technicians who will perform in-orbit inspection, maintenance, and repair jobs on malfunctioning satellites.

In 1977, NASA solicited candidates for shuttle pilots and mission specialists, and received more than eight thousand applications. These were first pared down to a list of two hundred, and then in January 1978 the space agency selected thirty-five new astronaut candidates. Fifteen were chosen in the pilot-

These six mission specialist/astronaut candidates are the first women to be named by NASA as astronaut candidates. They are *(left to right)* Margaret R. (Rhea) Seddon, Anna L. Fisher, Judith A. Resnik, Shannon W. Lucid, Sally K. Ride, and Kathryn D. Sullivan. The six women, along with the other candidates, were presented at Johnson Space Center on January 31, 1978.

astronaut category, and twenty as potential mission specialists, including, for the first time in the history of America's space program, six women. Among the women were two medical doctors, a biochemist, an electrical engineer, a physics research assistant, and a postgraduate student.

"One of the most rewarding things in our search for new astronauts was that we found that there are a large number of very highly qualified women in the United States who can meet the qualifications we set out," said Dr. Christopher Kraft, Director of NASA's Johnson Space Center. "As to their training, we don't propose they get any kind of different training than any of our other candidates."

In addition, three black men and one Japanese-American were chosen for the program. They were the first members of minority groups to be selected.

These candidates are now undergoing a two-year period of training and evaluation. They have been placed in responsible technical or scientific positions at NASA's Johnson Space Center, near Houston, Texas.

The training for the candidates includes all aspects of the shuttle's flight program. Pilots and mission specialists must know every system aboard the shuttle—how it works, what happens if it fails to operate, how it "interfaces" with other systems, how to operate equipment, etc. A lot of cross-training is involved, so that if one crew member becomes sick, for example, another member can step in to handle his or her assignments without affecting the success of the mission.

Final selection of pilots and mission specialists for actual shuttle flights will depend on their satisfactory completion of the two-year training and evaluation period. Once that selection has been made, each new crew member is expected to sign an agreement to serve NASA as an astronaut for a minimum period of five years.

It is unlikely that any of the thirty-five people selected in January 1978 will fly on the first few shuttle missions. These pilots and mission specialists will be chosen from the ranks of existing astronauts, who have been in shuttle training for several years. Once the shuttle becomes operational and the launch schedules are stepped up, the newer members will be added to the flight rosters.

Payload specialists will be chosen as needed, and in time for extensive training with other crew members for their specific flights. Already the finalists for the first Spacelab mission, which is tentatively scheduled for December 1980 or early 1981, have been named. Six Americans and four Europeans will compete for two research positions on that seven-day flight. One of the Americans is a woman—Ann Whitaker, a physicist from NASA's Marshall Space Flight Center in Huntsville, Alabama.

Although payload specialists are primarily responsible for the operation and management of the experiments or other payload elements to which they are assigned, they, too, will be thoroughly cross-trained. This will give them the capability to assist the mission specialist as necessary or to help other payload specialists in operating experiments.

They will man such support systems as instrument-pointing devices and scientific air locks, and they will learn how to run other orbiter equipment, such as hatches, food and hygiene systems, and the emergency systems.

The payload specialists do not have to be as knowledgeable in overall operations as the pilots or the mission specialists, but it will be important for them to train with other crew members for their specific flights. This intense prelaunch training may take from three to nine months before flight.

Training for all crew members will include lengthy sessions in mission simulators. These are advanced computerized models of the shuttle systems where many flight conditions in space can be closely duplicated for practice runs. Even emergency situations can be simulated to teach crew members how to react. Such training has proved invaluable during past manned space programs.

The space shuttle, then, opens up the possibility of space flight to a far broader spectrum of people. No longer is it essential to be a qualified jet pilot with a thousand or more hours of flight experience to qualify as a crew member, although astronaut-pilots will still need this capability.

Men and women in dozens of fields may qualify for future shuttle flights. Age and health restrictions, too, have been relaxed. Any otherwise qualified person of reasonably good health may apply. People in their twenties, thirties, forties, and even older may now have the opportunity to participate in one of the great adventures of our time.

6

Mission Versatility Is the Key

In August 1969, a large, multipurpose satellite, which cost tens of millions of dollars to design, build, and prepare for space flight, was successfully launched from the Kennedy Space Center. The 950-pound craft, called ATS-5 by NASA, was crammed full of sophisticated instruments and experiments that had taken scientists and engineers years to plan, research, and assemble.

ATS-5 carried new communications equipment for air-traffic control tests from space; an environmental measurement package that would gather data on earth pollution; microwave-communications gear; and other complex scientific experiments and expensive electronic machinery.

Shortly after the spacecraft was shoved into earth orbit by its powerful booster, something went wrong with the activating devices that controlled ATS-5 from the ground, and the entire spacecraft was rendered useless. An engineer on the spot could probably have fixed the malfunctioning parts in a few minutes. But as it was, officials on the ground were helpless. There was nothing they could do. Years of work and tens of millions of dollars went down the drain.

Once the space shuttle is operational, however, most such disasters will be eliminated. For the shuttle is designed to be able to maneuver onto the same orbital path as many satellites in space. Once it catches up with them in orbit, crew members will either retrieve the balky craft and return it to earth in the cargo section for repairs, or a specialist may be able to correct it on station in orbit.

In a study of 131 satellite failures over the years, 78 were related to faulty launches. These would be avoided with a reliable shuttle. Of the remaining 53 failures, the spacecraft payloads were either inoperable or erratic and could have been repaired in space or returned to earth if the shuttle had been available.

Such maintenance and repair jobs in space are only one of the many functions the shuttle will carry out. Its designed versatility, in fact, is one of the most important selling points of the program.

Here are some of the specific missions the shuttle will begin flying in the 1980s:

PLACEMENT OF SATELLITES

In a sense, the orbiter will serve as a sort of space truck, hauling satellites to be placed in earth orbit. As many as five different satellites may be carried up at one time. Each spacecraft will be serviced, checked out, and loaded aboard the orbiter.

The remote manipulator arm of a space-shuttle orbiter has just released its payload —a satellite and its propulsion stage—from the orbiter's cargo bay. The orbiter will be moved a safe distance away before ground control gives radio command signals to fire the orbiter's propulsion-stage engines.

In orbit, the specialists will give all satellite systems a final going over. After determining everything is ready, the crew will operate the payload-deployment system. This spindly mechanical arm, working like a giant crane, will lift the satellite from the cargo bay, move it away from the orbiter, and release it.

Final activation of the satellite will be by radio command, but the orbiter and its crew will stand by until the new satellite is operating satisfactorily before proceeding with the rest of the mission.

This type of satellite placement will save millions of dollars a year over present-day systems. For one thing, current spacecraft have to be designed with expensive backup parts for much of their critical equipment, so if one part fails in space, the backup part is activated. With the shuttle standing by, however, such duplication is not needed. If the satellite does not start performing properly, it can be retrieved and taken back to earth for necessary repairs.

Also, with satellites today, many of their systems, including computers, electronics, experiment packages, sensors, etc., have to be miniaturized at additional expense to fit within extremely tight weight limitations. This will be greatly relaxed on the shuttle, which can carry much heavier payloads into space comfortably.

RECOVERY OF SATELLITES

If a satellite fails in low earth orbit, or if it just stops operating because its energy supply has been expended, the orbiter will rendezvous with it in space, maneuver close to it, and the orbiter's remote manipulator arm will reach out and grab it. The mute satellite will then be lowered into the cargo bay and locked into place for the return trip home. On earth, engineers can repair any malfunctioning parts, recharge the energy supply, or equip the spacecraft with fresh systems and parts. It then can be returned to its position in space on a later shuttle flight. Tremendous cost savings will be made by refurbishing satellites rather than having to build new ones for each mission.

PLACEMENT OF FREE-FLYING LABORATORIES IN SPACE

In addition to the ferrying of satellites and spacecraft to and from orbit, the shuttle will also be called upon to place free-flying scientific laboratories in space. Too large and too expensive to be launched by conventional rocket systems, such labs will fit neatly into the cargo bay of the orbiter.

One such payload will be a huge space telescope that will serve as a permanent international observatory in orbit for the study of the universe. By operating above the earth's obscuring atmospheric haze, the sun, the solar system, the galaxy and other galaxies will be observed with much greater coverage, sensitivity, and resolution than was ever before possible.

In earth orbit, mission specialists prepare to release a space telescope from the huge payload bay of the space-shuttle orbiter. The space telescope is scheduled to be placed into orbit in the mid 1980s.

With the space telescope in operation, astronomers will be able to

• Compare the earth's atmosphere with those of other planets.
• Explore the process of planet and star formation.
• Study extremely powerful distant energy sources, including quasars, believed to be the most remote observable objects in the universe, and pulsars, thought to be fast-spinning neutron stars.
• Locate and investigate black holes, believed to be the final stage in the collapse of a dying massive star whose material is so tightly packed that not even light waves are able to escape.
• Study cosmology, the structure and origin of the universe.

The space telescope is to be launched on a shuttle flight in the early 1980s, and will be periodically revisited on subsequent flights for maintenance. Thus scientists consider that it will be usable for the rest of this century.

Another free-flying lab to be placed in orbit by the shuttle is the Long Duration Exposure Facility, or LDEF. This is a very large open-work cylindrical structure, actually a 12-sided regular polygon. It is 30 feet long, 14 feet in diameter, and it will fit snugly inside the orbiter's cargo bay.

A space telescope in earth orbit after being released from the space-shuttle orbiter. The orbiter will periodically visit the telescope for maintenance, making the space telescope usable for the rest of this century.

In effect, the LDEF is a framework that will house seventy-six trays—each of which will contain a technical or scientific experiment. Each tray will be 50 inches long, 38 inches wide, with a depth of either 3, 6, or 12 inches, depending on the experiment. NASA has encouraged experimenters from NASA centers, other government agencies, the Department of Defense, major universities and colleges, research institutes, and American industry to participate in this phase of the shuttle program. Also, scientists from France, the Netherlands, and England are preparing experiments to fly aboard LDEF.

A wide range of experiments will be included in the initial LDEF flight, which will be hauled into space on one of the first operational shuttle missions. These will include such subjects as astrophysics, life sciences, lunar and planetary studies, solar-terrestrial studies, and upper-atmospheric physics.

About 20 percent of the experiment space on the first LDEF flight will contain micrometeoroid-detection panels, designed to measure the number and variety of tiny meteoroid particles in

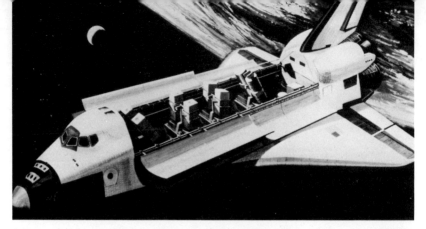

A space-shuttle orbiter in earth orbit, with its payload bay doors open showing a payload for scientific experiments.

earth orbit. Some scientists believe that most of these micrometeoroids are derived from comets. If so, their chemical makeup would be of great importance, because comets are generally considered to be relatively unaltered objects in space and may hold answers to how the solar system was formed.

The first LDEF will be placed in a 270-mile circular orbit and left there for from six to twelve months. It will then be retrieved by a later shuttle flight and brought back to earth. Experiments will be removed and returned to the experts who designed them for detailed study.

The cylindrical structure itself will be refurbished and prepared for another mission with a new assortment of experiments. Following the first LDEF flight, NASA will set up a "marketing" type of office at the Kennedy Space Center where interested experimenters can apply for tray space and pay for use of that space.

THE "GETAWAY SPECIAL"

Most of the experiments for LDEF will be relatively complex packages with sophisticated, sensitive equipment that is very expensive. But NASA also is planning to provide a unique opportunity for individuals, companies, and institutions to conduct experiments in space at moderate cost. The name of this interesting program is Small Self-Contained Payloads, or the "Getaway Special."

Experiments in this program must weigh 200 pounds or less and be self-contained in a packaged compartment measuring not more than 5 cubic feet in volume. Costs for ferrying this type of experiment to and from space may vary from about $3,000 to $5,000 for the smallest package—1.5 cubic feet—to from $7,000 to $10,000 for larger ones.

Experiments may cover a wide range of subject matter. NASA says only that the payload must be related to a "scientific or technological objective." These experiments will be flown on a space-available basis—that is, NASA will fly as many as there is room for on each mission.

There are few restrictions on who can participate. NASA says any responsible person, organization, or institution can take advantage of the Getaway Special program. Conceivably, junior high and high school students can take part. During the Skylab program in the early 1970s, NASA and the National Association of Teachers of Science sponsored a project encouraging talented high school students in the United States to submit science-related experiments and demonstrations for possible flight aboard Skylab in orbit.

From more than thirty-four hundred entries, nineteen finalists were selected, and many of their experiments were included in the three-flight Skylab program. One of the most famous was the student who proposed sending a spider into space to see if it could weave a web in the weightless environment—it did. Another student suggested using infrared cameras to observe volcanoes on earth from space, noting that an increase in heat as measured by such detection might prove to signal a potential eruption.

It is possible that schools or youth science organizations will sponsor similar student experiments for participation in the shuttle's Getaway Special program in the 1980s.

WALKS IN SPACE

Astronaut Ed White participated in the first extravehicular activity, or EVA, during his Gemini 4 flight in 1965 when he stepped outside his spacecraft and, connected by a life-supporting tether line, "walked" in space. He was so fascinated by the experience that ground controllers had to order him to go back inside the Gemini spacecraft. On the shuttle flights of the 1980s, such EVA will serve many useful purposes.

On these excursions, which may last up to six hours apiece, astronauts could inspect and possibly repair the orbiter, if need be, in much the same way as astronauts Conrad and Kerwin did on the first Skylab flight. They also may be called upon to

• Install, remove, and transfer film cassettes, material samples, protective covers, and instruments.
• Operate such equipment as assembly tools, cameras, and cleaning devices.
• Store fluids and connect or disconnect electrical units.
• Repair, replace, calibrate, reposition, and inspect modular equipment, antennas, and instruments on the spacecraft or payload.

The shuttle has been designed to be launched both from the east coast of the United States, at the Kennedy Space Center, and from the west coast at Vandenberg Air Force Base, California, between Los Angeles and San Francisco. Most launches will be made to a relatively low orbit.

With the advent of the shuttle transportation system, astronauts will be able to inspect and repair the orbiter. The orbital technicians here are equipped with extra-vehicular-mobility units (space suits and backpacks) and manned maneuvering units for transportation.

The majority of missions will begin from the Kennedy Space Center. Most of these will be for satellites and spacecraft that operate in orbits around or near the equator. But, starting in 1983, flights from Vandenberg will be made to place satellites in polar orbit. Such orbits cover more land areas of the world and will be used for such missions as the Landsat earth-resource surveillance program and Department of Defense missions, where regions of strategic military importance can better be covered.

It is necessary to launch into polar orbit from the west coast for safety reasons. To reach polar orbit from the Kennedy Center would require the shuttle to fly over land, such as Cuba, en route to space. So for safety purposes, NASA prefers only to fly over water wherever possible. This can be achieved from Vandenberg out over the Pacific Ocean. Launches for other orbital flights can be made from Kennedy without flying over land.

DELIVERY OF PAYLOADS
THAT USE PROPULSION SYSTEMS

While the shuttle is extremely versatile as a space transportation system, it does have limitations. Its design restricts it to near-earth orbital flights. Many satellites today, and about half of those planned for the future, must achieve much higher orbits to do their jobs effectively. Communications satellites, for example, must be placed in what is called a geosynchronous orbit, about 22,300 miles above earth. At this altitude, they travel in orbit at the same speed as the earth rotates, so they can remain in space in a "stationary" position over a specific area on earth, such as the Atlantic Ocean or Europe. Three satellites positioned at 120-degree intervals in geosynchronous orbit can cover the entire globe except for small areas around the poles.

Other satellites must be launched into highly elliptical orbits with wide-ranging arcs that swing near the earth at times, then travel far distances away. Also, some space missions are destined to reach neighboring planets, or to venture deep into the solar system and beyond, such as the Mariner flights scheduled to orbit the planet Jupiter in the mid-1980s.

For these higher orbital flights and deep space probes, the shuttle will carry both spacecraft and propulsion systems, or engines, into earth orbit. There they will be deployed much like other payloads. The entire system—spacecraft and propulsion system—will be thoroughly checked out and readied for launch. Guidance information will be updated.

The orbiter then will move a safe distance away before ground control gives radio command signals to fire the engines that will boost the spacecraft to its ultimate destination.

Initially a solid propulsion stage, being developed by the Department of Defense, will be used in such orbit launches. It is

The Teleoperator Retrieval System (TRS), to be used in conjunction with the space shuttle in the early 1980s, approaches a satellite for docking and retrieval. This system will be used to survey, stabilize, and maneuver payloads in low earth orbit.

called the Inertial Upper Stage, or IUS. At present, the IUS is not reusable, but there are plans to make fully reusable propulsion stages in the future.

Again there are multiple advantages in using the shuttle to carry out these missions. Large, expensive rocket systems needed to launch the spacecraft from earth can be eliminated. And should something malfunction during their launch from orbit, the craft and propulsion stage can be retrieved for inspection and possible immediate repair. If the repairs cannot be done on station, the entire payload—satellite and stage—can be returned to earth for refurbishment.

These then are some of the primary mission capabilities of the shuttle as envisioned today. But the beauty of this new space transportation system is that it is not necessarily limited to uses that can be currently forecast. Once flights become commonplace and experience has been gained, many new and now unforeseen uses will undoubtedly be found to take advantage of the shuttle's relatively low mission cost and all-around versatility.

7

Partners from Overseas

One of the great intangible benefits of America's space program is the international goodwill that has been created through cooperative programs involving many of the world's nations. Since its creation in 1958, NASA has entered into hundreds of agreements for international space projects. These have included orbiting foreign satellites with United States rockets; flying experiments of overseas scientists on American spacecraft; and participating in more than six hundred scientific rocket experiments from locations all over the globe.

When, in 1972, NASA launched the first Landsat satellite to survey the earth's resources from space, it carried more than three hundred experiments designed by experts in the United States, thirty-seven foreign countries, and two United Nations groups. And the information gathered by Landsats, weather satellites, and other spacecraft is shared with most of the nations of the world. Through the communications satellites launched by the United States, historic events can be transmitted live to the far corners of the earth.

Following the Apollo landings on the moon in 1969 and the early 1970s, NASA sponsored a program enabling sixty-five of the world's foremost scientists in eighteen countries to analyze geological samples brought back from the lunar surface. And the data they uncovered while performing physical, chemical, mineralogical, and biological experiments was openly published and circulated.

Perhaps the single most-publicized joint venture in space was the 1975 United States—Soviet Union mission during which American astronauts in an Apollo spacecraft and Russian cosmonauts in a Soyuz spacecraft joined up in earth orbit. They flew with their crafts linked together, performing a variety of important experiments.

The shuttle, in the 1980s, will open a new era of international cooperation in space. It offers advantages in volume, weight, preparation, environmental and cost advantages that no conventional launcher system—either America's or any other nation's—can match. It therefore will become the preferred means of getting into orbit for any country wishing to use space.

At an early stage in the planning of the shuttle program, NASA sought to encourage participation by member nations of the European Space Agency (ESA). In August 1973, NASA signed an agreement with ten ESA countries whereby they would fund, build, and operate a space laboratory to be flown in earth orbit aboard the shuttle. The countries were Belgium, Denmark,

A full-scale mockup of Spacelab. There are two main sections—the open pallet *(front),* which exposes materials and equipment directly to space; and a pressurized laboratory module *(back)* where scientists work. Spacelab is designed to fit in the payload-bay area of the space-shuttle orbiter.

West Germany, France, Italy, the Netherlands, Spain, Switzerland, the United Kingdom, and Austria. Since then, Ireland has been added to the program, and although Sweden and Austria are members of ESA, they are not participating directly in Spacelab. The development cost of Spacelab has been estimated at close to $600 million.

As the shuttle design evolved through the early 1970s, so, too, did Spacelab. Its two principal parts are a pressurized module, or section, which provides a laboratory where scientists can work comfortably; and an open pallet, which exposes materials and equipment directly to space.

The laboratory module has two segments. One is called the core segment. It houses a number of supporting subsystems, such as data-processing equipment and utilities. It also contains such lab fixtures as floor-mounted racks and workbenches and supplies. The second or experiment segment is used to provide more working lab space.

One configuration of Spacelab in the payload bay of the space shuttle. At the fore end is the pressurized laboratory module, connected to the shuttle-orbiter airlock by a crew-access tunnel. At the other end are two pallet sections on which are mounted various scientific instruments. The equipment on the pallets is operated by remote control from the laboratory module.

Each of the two segments is pressurized to enable experimenters to work inside them without having to wear space suits. Each segment is a cylinder 13.5 feet in diameter and 9 feet long. A tunnel connects the pressurized laboratory with the cabin of the shuttle orbiter.

The open-pallet area not only is a platform for mounting experiment instruments, but it also can cool equipment, provide electrical power, and furnish connections for commanding and acquiring data from the experiments.

The individual pallets—each of which is 10 feet long, and as many as five of which may be flown on any one mission—are designed for large experiments requiring direct exposure to the space environment, or needing unobstructed or broad fields of view. For example, this equipment may include telescopes, antennas, and sensors such as radiometers and radars.

The entire configuration, including core and experiment segments and the pallets, has a maximum length of 23 feet. This fits compactly within the orbiter's cargo-bay area.

Because of its modular design, Spacelab can easily be modified for a variety of missions, and, like the orbiter itself, Spacelab is reusable. Each module is built for at least fifty space missions. From one to four payload specialists will travel on each Spacelab flight. They will closely coordinate their activities in space with experimenters on the ground and with the shuttle's crew.

Experiments to be carried aboard Spacelab are designed to advance man's scientific knowledge and to create new technology that will benefit humans on earth. For instance, payload specialists will test and calibrate sensors and other instruments that later will be used in automated earth observation satellites. In the process, the specialists are expected to gather a variety of information useful in transportation, urban planning, pollution control, farming, fishing, navigation, weather forecasting, and prospecting for new mineral and energy sources.

In astronomy, observations are planned to add to knowledge about the sun and its interactions with earth's environment. Comets and novas will be studied, and observations of high-energy radiation from the far corners of the universe will be made. Such radiation, which does not for the most part pass through earth's protective atmosphere and therefore cannot be studied from the ground, includes gamma rays, X rays, and ultraviolet light.

But scientists believe this radiation is very important, and can best be studied from a platform in orbit such as Spacelab will offer. Locked in this radiation are answers to many questions about the nature, origin, and evolution of celestial phenomena and basic knowledge about our solar system and planet.

In the life sciences, studies of man and of other living things in space have indicated significant metabolic changes resulting from the absence of gravity. Continued study from specialists on

Spacelab is expected to increase understanding of these changes. This will add to our knowledge of life processes and contribute to the advancement of medicine.

Another important field of study will be in biomedicine. The stable, gravity-free environment of space has demonstrated distinct advantages in separating and purifying biological particles. Some of these processes cannot be done on earth because of gravity problems. In orbit, however, there will be increased opportunities for removal from vaccines of impurities that cause undesirable side effects, and for isolating specific cells or antibodies for treatment of disease.

Spacelab will advance the science of industrial technology, too. As proven on the Skylab flights of the early 1970s, zero gravity conditions in space create an environment that lends itself to the manufacture of new alloys and other composite materials that are uniquely strong, lightweight, and temperature resistant. Such environment has also proved favorable to the growing of very large crystals of high purity for use in electronics—and to the creating of pure glass, free of container contamination, for optical, electronic, and laser uses.

On the first Spacelab mission, investigations will be conducted in stratospheric and upper-atmosphere physics, material processing, space-plasma physics, biology, medicine, astronomy, solar physics, earth observations, and in technology areas, such as thermodynamics and lubrication.

Worldwide reaction to Spacelab has been highly enthusiastic. When NASA and the European Space Agency issued invitations for experiments to be flown on the first Spacelab mission in the 1980s, more than 2,000 scientists from all over the world responded. From these, the experiments of 222 investigators from fifteen nations have been selected for the initial flight. Payload specialists—men and women from many different countries—will conduct experiments in space for periods ranging from seven to thirty days, before returning to earth aboard the orbiter. Following each flight, Spacelab will be removed from the cargo bay. The experiments will be dismounted and distributed to scientists for further analysis, while Spacelab is readied for its next mission.

Aside from the enormous amount of scientific knowledge to be gained via Spacelab—much of which will be applied to improving life on earth—perhaps an even more significant result will be the great step forward this program will achieve toward global cooperation in space. NASA has called Spacelab an "outstanding example of how peoples of many lands can unite their talents and resources in future space projects to benefit humanity."

The official emblem of Spacelab, a cooperative venture between the National Aeronautics and Space Administration (NASA) and the European Space Agency (ESA). The figures at center represent scientists working inside the Spacelab module.

8

Orbital Command Post

While there are seldom any public announcements or any publicity about them, the United States and the Soviet Union launch dozens of satellites into orbit each year for military purposes. Actually, development of United States Department of Defense rockets and spacecraft coincides with the earliest days of the American space program. The nation's first satellite, Explorer I, was launched January 31, 1958, by a modified Redstone booster originally developed for the Army.

In the early 1960s, Redstones were used to start astronauts Alan Shepard and Virgil "Gus" Grissom on their short, suborbital space flights. Redesigned Air Force Atlas rockets sent John Glenn, Scott Carpenter, Wally Schirra, and Gordon Cooper into earth-orbital missions. Air Force Titan missiles propelled Gemini astronauts into orbit immediately preceding the Apollo moon-landing program.

Modified versions of Atlas, Titan, and Thor rockets have been used for years to launch a variety of NASA satellites for weather observation, communications, and scientific missions. The air force's Agena vehicle helped send the first spacecraft on long-distance flights past the planets Venus and Mars.

Today the Department of Defense, or DOD, views space as a new environment, a new outpost from which to continue the job of protecting national interests. The United States Air Force has the responsibility for the development and launching of military space boosters for DOD, and is the principal agency for space development programs concerned with the nation's defense.

This is the Block 5-D weather satellite, launched by the Air Force for the Defense Department in 1975. The Block 5-D provides weather data to U.S. forces worldwide.

Space flights for military purposes are important because of the tremendous area of earth coverage possible from a satellite. These capabilities are far superior for information-gathering assignments that require broad coverage, such as communications relay, weather and cloud-cover observations, navigation data, surveillance over land and water, and detection of foreign-missile launches.

The air force, for example, has developed a system of early-warning satellites designed to detect the launching of any intercontinental ballistic missile (ICBM) or sea-launched ballistic missile (SLBM). The same satellites are used to report on atmospheric nuclear explosions.

These early-warning or photographic reconnaissance spacecraft serve two basic purposes. First, they take panoramic photos from orbit to detect evidence of new construction and such installations of military interest as airfields, missile sites, and strategic targets. Second, high-quality, close-up photos of specific sites can be taken. New camera and sensing systems are capable of photographing objects as small as a foot high from orbital altitudes of a hundred or more miles.

Such highly sensitive equipment can maintain a constant vigil on the world's major powers. This assures against the repetition of a surprise military attack, such as occurred at Pearl Harbor at the start of World War II, even if nuclear missiles are used. These electronic "spies in the sky" can also warn against the unauthorized buildup of weapons bases, such as occurred in Cuba in the early 1960s. Furthermore, these surveillance satellites can contribute to international arms-control agreements between the world's major powers. A nation is not likely to violate such agreements by building secret bases if such bases can be seen and reported the instant they are begun.

Communications satellites are important to the national defense program. Shown here is the Navy-sponsored fleet satellite communications system spacecraft—FLTSATCOM—in flight. This system provides worldwide, high-priority, ultra-high-frequency communications between many aircraft, ships, submarines, ground stations, the strategic air command, and the presidential command networks.

Communications satellites also are important to the national defense program. Through them, information can instantly be relayed over continental distances to armed forces on the land, sea, or in the air. During the Vietnam War, such satellites were used to transmit high-speed digital data from South Vietnam to the Pentagon, near Washington. This system allowed military strategists and analysts to view high-quality reconnaissance photographs of battle zones minutes after they were taken. The North Atlantic Treaty Organization (NATO) uses a communications-satellite system to keep its member nations instantly alerted to military matters.

The United States Navy pioneered in the use of space for navigational purposes. This type of satellite can give ships at sea their exact position at any time of day or night in any kind of weather. Not only is this important for naval strategic purposes, but also it provides a system that can precisely pinpoint ships in distress for rescue purposes.

The Department of Defense has long used space for the collection and swift dispatch of weather information vital to the placement and movement of military forces on land, sea, or in the air.

Still other defense missions in space are highly classified, and there is no published information about them available. But it is known that orbital systems are necessary to deter other nations from ever attempting to use space as a launching pad for directing nuclear or other weapons toward earth, or from using spatial weapons to destroy other satellites in orbit.

It is obvious, then, that there will be an ever-increasing need for defense satellites in earth orbit be they used for surveillance, communications, navigational, meteorological, or other purposes.

Over the past two decades DOD has launched hundreds of satellites into space at great cost to American taxpayers. And, like NASA flights, these missions have resulted in the discarding of rocket boosters and other expensive hardware and equipment after only one use.

After several years of study the air force, in the early 1970s, concluded that the most promising way significantly to cut costs would be through the use of reusable launch vehicles. The study further pointed out that additional savings could be made by being able to recover and reuse satellites and to conduct in-orbit maintenance on those systems that developed defects.

The most logical answer: use of NASA's space shuttle.

From the earliest design stages of the shuttle program, air force experts have worked very closely with NASA and with the contractor engineers and technicians to help define a system that would meet many defense requirements in addition to the other missions to be performed.

The air force also pledged full support of the program, offering its years of aerospace expertise developed and refined through the testing, launching, and operation of hundreds of missiles, rockets, and spacecraft. The air force has extensive experience in operating, testing, and maintaining large aircraft, and in refitting and providing ground support for them. Much of this knowledge can be directly applied to the shuttle, for in a number of ways it will be flown and operated like a large aircraft.

Projections are that up to 30 percent of the shuttle's annual payload capacity may be devoted to defense missions, once the system is fully operational. This means that in the 1980s and 1990s as many as twenty flights each year may be for military purposes.

The majority of these flights, beginning in 1983, will be launched from Vandenberg Air Force Base, California, between Los Angeles and San Francisco. The Department of Defense is charged with the responsibility for preparing the Vandenberg launch site for shuttle flights.

Defense missions aboard the shuttle will be similar to those on other flights. Satellites will be flown to earth orbit for release there, or for transfer, via the Inertial Upper Stage, to higher orbits. Satellites may be repaired on station or retrieved for return to earth. Film and other data may be picked up from spacecraft in orbit for detailed study on the ground. And, conceivably, military experts on occasion will fly to space aboard the shuttle for firsthand observations and analysis.

Defense technology helps the United States to preserve its freedom and to protect world peace. The space shuttle will enable the Department of Defense to continue this vital task more efficiently, more reliably, and at a greatly reduced cost to the taxpayer.

"I am convinced that because the United States has been a major sea power, we have contributed to open use of the seas by all nations," says former U.S. Congressman Olin Teague of Texas, part chairman of the House Science and Astronautics Committee. "I am equally convinced that only so long as the United States is a major space power will the free use of space be available to all mankind."

9

Benefits on Earth

NASA officials have estimated that a fully operational shuttle system will save approximately $1 billion a year between the years of 1980 and 1991.

But even with all these savings, the shuttle represents a multibillion-dollar program that must be paid for, in large part, by American taxpayers. This raises some key questions. What are we getting for our money? Is the shuttle program worth this great expense? How are we, living on earth, going to benefit?

The answers are all around us. Yet already we take so many of them for granted that we do not recognize them as spin-off dividends from space technology.

Consider, for example, the revolutionary advances made in the

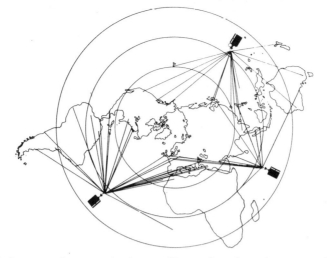

A global system of communication satellites and earth stations now exists. Three Intelsat satellites, positioned 120 degrees apart in synchronous orbit 22,300 miles up, can cover the entire earth.

field of communications over the past few years. With just three satellites, positioned 120 degrees apart in synchronous orbits 22,-300 miles up, the entire earth can be covered. Historic, athletic, news, and other events originating on one continent can be beamed instantaneously to countries on the other side of the world. In fact, today's sophisticated communications satellites can transmit up to twenty simultaneous color-television programs across oceans from continent to continent.

Each spacecraft also carries thousands of telephone and tele-type circuits which can speed important government, business, and other messages to distant points of the globe in seconds. Such services not only are better and faster, but they also save money for users. The cost of a three-minute phone call from London, England, to the east coast of the United States has been lowered by more than 40 percent because of the improved efficiency of satellite communications over transoceanic cables.

Data and facsimile transmission via satellite is marking a new era in business communications. A newspaper edited in New York, for example, may send editorial copy and advertising via a satellite to its printing plant a thousand miles or more away at the rate of a page every three minutes. International companies can transmit the results of important meetings to overseas managers or stockholders at the speed of light. Indeed, many such meetings may be beamed live worldwide.

In education, courses, lectures, and seminars taught by leading experts can be transmitted live by satellite to unlimited numbers of students in classrooms and training centers hundreds or thousands of miles apart. New surgical techniques being used in open-heart surgery in Houston, Texas, may be observed during the operation by doctors all across North America and in Europe and Asia.

Another spin-off benefit, which today is taken for granted, is the greatly improved science of weather tracking and forecasting made possible by meteorological satellites. NASA estimates that since the first such satellite was orbited in 1960, more than a hundred thousand lives and countless hundreds of millions of dollars in property, in the United States alone, have been saved through advanced warning of hurricanes, tornadoes, and other storms. These figures increase greatly when the many other nations around the world with whom America shares its satellite weather data are taken into consideration.

But even these savings may prove small compared to what may be accomplished in the near future. With new developments in meteorological instruments and the placement of professional weather observers in orbit on the shuttle, experts believe accurate long-range forecasts of from five days to two weeks will be possible. Such preknowledge made available to farmers, operators of shipping lines, commercial fishermen, businessmen and women, water- and land-resource managers, and others undoubtedly will save incalculable billions of dollars in the years to come.

This is Landsat-2, the second earth-resources satellite, placed into orbit on January 2, 1975. Data collected from its camera and scanner systems is used to conduct investigations in geology, hydrology, agriculture, land-use planning, and marine and water resources.

Immeasurable benefits are being derived, too, through the use of such earth-surveillance satellites as Landsat. Constantly circling earth with all-seeing electronic sensors, these versatile spacecraft can forecast agricultural crop yields and spot crop diseases from space sooner than a farmer can on his own land.

Consider the potential savings in agriculture alone. Losses caused by plant disease in the United States are estimated at $3.7 billion annually. And the losses caused by pests add up to another $3.8 billion. That's $7.5 billion a year in agricultural losses in the United States alone. With satellite systems in space, we can tell the type of crop in each field, the size of the field, the vigor of the crop, the probable yield, and the identity of such damaging agents as blight or insect infestation. By applying this information on a routine operational basis in the shuttle era, billions of dollars in savings can annually be realized.

Such satellites can also search the remote hidden places of the world for new mineral, oil, and energy sources. They can spot and pinpoint forest fires and sight potential earthquake locations.

They can track migratory wildlife and zero in on large schools of fish in the sea. They can report faster and more accurately than can be done on earth the damage caused by such natural disasters as floods and large storms. They can monitor timber reserves and measure snow depths.

The least-tapped natural resource on earth is the ocean. The Bureau of Commercial Fisheries, in cooperation with the Naval Oceanographic Office, is already investigating how remote sensing from space aboard the shuttle can be used to survey ocean resources, ocean surface temperatures, current patterns, biological productivity, the sea state, sea ice, and shoaling processes.

All of this information from space helps the human race to manage better this planet's limited resources. How much money is this one phase of the space program saving? It is difficult to measure in terms of dollars. But the sighting from orbit of just one new potential source of energy alone, whether oil or mineral, would have tremendous economic impact. The early detection of a major crop disease could save that crop and thus provide food for thousands of people. A single report of one winter's abnormal snowfall could later result in saving thousands of lives and millions of dollars in property through early flood-warning preparations.

And when experts—geologists and oceanographers, cartographers and land-use managers, hydrologists, and forestry and wildlife specialists—are sent into orbit for firsthand observation from the shuttle, in coordination with the steady stream of satellite data, even more benefits will be forthcoming.

How, too, can the value of having a cleaner earth with fresher air and water be rated in terms of dollars? Proven technology has demonstrated that the extent of water and air pollution, and sometimes their sources, can be established by space photogra-

This photo, taken from the Landsat-1 satellite in 1973, highlights very graphically the water pollution in Lake Erie near Detroit.

phy. The distribution patterns of air pollution, in fact, can be tracked over great distances, and from such data scientists can distinguish concentration levels of smog and other pollutants, as well as the rate of movement and the rate of dispersion.

When such information is gathered and reported back to earth on a routine basis, as will be possible during the shuttle era, pollution alerts can be given well in advance of approaching clouds of contaminants. Sensitive electronic eyes in space also can detect the dumping of effluents, even thermal discharges, into streams, rivers, lakes, and seas. And infrared equipment will be able to discern industrial polluters who attempt to mask illegal discharges under the cloak of darkness. Such data will greatly aid local, state, and federal environmental-protection agencies in pinpointing violators.

NASA says one pollution-mapping satellite can cover the entire United States in about five hundred photographs, whereas cameras carried in high-altitude airplanes would use about half a million frames to cover the same area. What would take years to monitor by air can be monitored from space in a few days.

A new satellite system, to become operational in the mid-1980s, will lead to the day of the automated ship at sea. The system will be made up of navigation satellites positioned at strategic orbital points that will afford global coverage on earth. Using the system, ships will leave ports with small crews, primarily electronics specialists who will operate and maintain computers and other sophisticated equipment. Satellite position information will be fed directly into shipboard computers, and vessels will stay on a perfect prescribed course to their final destination.

To be flown to orbit aboard the shuttle, the Department of Defense's NAVSTAR global-positioning system will insure instantaneous, all-weather navigational coverage for users throughout the world. Twenty-four such satellites will broadcast continuous navigational information, enabling a properly equipped user to determine his position within tens of feet; his speed within a tenth of a mile per hour; and the time within a millionth of a second.

How will such incredibly precise data directly benefit human beings? Former NASA official Charles W. Mathews says the maritime shipping industry alone could save hundreds of millions of dollars a year through optimum-time routing of ships, improved scheduling of ship arrivals and unloading, and more efficient use of personnel and equipment through improved ability to route, schedule, and predict ship-arrival times.

But an even greater benefit of a working navigational satellite system will be in human safety. Collisions at sea because of fog and other foul-weather conditions will be all but eliminated through the use of exact, up-to-the-second position data made

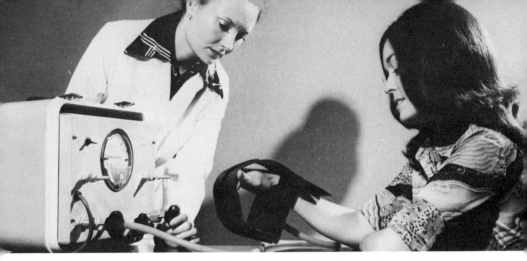

A spinoff from airflow-control technology, this pneumatically operated mitt helps rehabilitate the fingers of paralyzed or badly burned hands. Customary treatment requires a trained therapist to work the fingers for long periods daily, a painful and tedious process for the patient. The mitt flexes the fingers automatically, thus enabling the patient to conduct his own therapy and to stop the pain whenever he wishes by turning off the machine.

possible by satellite. And for people in trouble at sea, search-and-rescue craft will be able to zero in for speedy rescue on a precise location, regardless of weather conditions.

More down to earth, the spin-off benefits having medical applications have forged scores of important breakthroughs advancing the art of patient care and treatment. Space technology has fostered new, improved, and miniaturized heart pacemakers; electronic sensor systems, which enable a single nurse at one central location to monitor the heartbeats and other vital signs of dozens of patients; and electronic sight switches allow quadriplegics to operate wheelchairs by voice control. These represent just a small sampling of the space-spawned technology that already has been put to use in hospitals and health-care centers across the United States.

Even so, experts contend that what has been learned and applied to date is minor in respect to the medical knowledge that will be derived during the shuttle era.

There also is a long list of safety improvements on earth as a direct result of NASA space-program efforts. These include greatly improved fireproof apparel and fire-retardant or non-flammable foams, paints, fabrics, and glass-fiber laminates. Grooved highways make driving safer during wet weather, and NASA-developed antifogging compounds are being used in automotive windshields and in helmet visors worn by motorcyclists, firemen, and others.

With safety a primary consideration in the shuttle-program planning, there will undoubtedly be in the years ahead a continuing fallout to earth of new and better ideas for safety systems and devices.

As the most advanced transportation system ever conceived and developed by man, the shuttle will inevitably inspire further advancements in land, sea, and air transportation on earth. Space technology already has keyed design of some of the nation's most modern rapid-transit systems, such as BART (Bay Area Rapid Transportation) in San Francisco, and computerized passenger- and freight-information systems. Currently under study is an air-traffic-control satellite system which could virtually eliminate the chance of in-air collisions, and provide such added services as weather advisories, search-and-rescue data, and passenger telephone service.

More easily identifiable to the American consumer are the space-technology spin-offs that have improved products in and around the home. Freeze-dried foods, thermal cooking pins, heat-resistant coatings in cookware, digital clocks, and long-lasting batteries are just a selective handful of such benefits that quickly come to mind.

Solar-heating units and solar-cell arrays, which are fast becoming popular sources of energy for homes, offices, and other build-

Exits of Boston's Exeter Street Theater are lighted by Multi-Mode electronic lights, commercial spinoffs from a lighting system developed for NASA's Apollo and Skylab manned spacecraft. Advantages of Multi-Mode lights stem from the qualities demanded for spacecraft use: high light output with low energy drain, compactness, light weight, and high reliability.

ings, are additional examples of space-to-earth benefits. Many experiments to be carried into orbit by shuttle are being designed to advance our knowledge greatly in these and other important energy areas.

These, then, are some of the answers to the question, "What is the space program doing for the benefit of me here on earth?" Benefits from past and present space efforts have already worked their way into our daily lives, to a far greater extent that most of us realize. We have seen examples of how hundreds of millions and perhaps billions of dollars and countless lives can and are being saved each year through the direct, down-to-earth application of space technology. We have seen how these technological "tools" can and are being used effectively not only to preserve and manage earth's precious resources and environment, and to exploit its hidden riches, but also to enhance the quality of life for all earth's inhabitants.

But what has been gained to date is only the preamble. The shuttle era will open up an entire new book of earthly benefits for all mankind.

10

Costs and Critics

In the year 1491, a Spanish group called the Talavera Commission ruled that a proposed venture by a brash young master mariner named Christopher Columbus was "impossible, vain, and worthy of rejection." Fortunately, the group was overruled by Queen Isabella, who authorized Columbus's request to sail west across the Atlantic Ocean. Otherwise, the course of our history might well have been dramatically changed.

The point is, there have been critics of radically progressive new ideas and programs throughout civilization. Many leading Americans criticized the Louisiana Purchase as a waste of taxpayers' money. The same was true in 1867 when Secretary of State Seward paid $7.2 million for Alaska.

When the Wright brothers began experimenting in the sand dunes of eastern North Carolina at the beginning of this century, they were laughed at. Robert Goddard, one of the fathers of modern rocketry, was driven to experiment in the barren waste-lands of New Mexico to save himself and his family from being harassed by those who accused him of playing with toys.

But critics are not always shortsighted and ill informed. They often perform very important and necessary functions. There were many critics of the Apollo moon-landing program, for exam-ple. They contended that the United States committed too much money to conduct a crash program at a time when such funds could have been better spent on more down-to-earth problems, such as poverty, hunger, protection of the environment, and other terrestrial concerns.

And historians may agree that such critics had a point: that the manned lunar landings could have been accomplished far more economically had not the United States been in a race with the Soviet Union to see who would get to the moon first.

Today there are many critics of the space program, in general, and of the shuttle, in particular. And these critics include some of America's most distinguished and honored citizens, such as United States senators and congressmen and award-winning scientists. In fact, Vice President Walter Mondale, when he was a senator from Minnesota, was one of the shuttle program's earliest and most vocal critics.

It is worthwhile to examine and evaluate some of these criti-cisms and arguments.

A close examination of federal spending over the past few years refutes the argument that the space program diverts money that could be better spent on more pressing problems. For example, in 1969, at the time of the first moon landing, the federal government spent more than $65 billion for what were termed "social action" programs. These included welfare, health, veterans' benefits and services, education, and community development and housing. That same year just over $4 billion was budgeted for space. In 1970 more than $75 billion was funded for social-action programs and only $3.7 billion for NASA. In the 1970s the ratio has broadened even more.

Nearly half the national budget is allotted to domestic programs related to human and physical needs on earth, while less than 1.5 percent of it is spent on space. Those who back the space program make the point that the social problems confronting this nation today are not very likely to be wiped out, or even significantly reduced, by adding 1.5 percent to a budget that already includes nearly half of every tax dollar.

Furthermore, these space proponents contend that even if the space budget was wiped out completely, there is no assurance that the $3 billion to $4 billion annually allotted to space would be spent on social needs.

Another common argument has been that we waste money by spending it in space. The answer to that is, simply, that not a penny is spent *in* space. Rockets may launch satellites into orbit or spacecraft to the planets, but every piece of that hardware was designed, developed, and manufactured on earth. More than 90 percent of all federal funds budgeted for the space program have been spent in the United States. The economic impact of these funds, flowing from NASA to major contractors to the smallest subcontractor, affects thousands of companies and helps employ hundreds of thousands of workers in all fifty states.

There are nearly ten thousand subcontractors and supplier firms participating in the shuttle program. They are located at sites stretching from San Diego, California, to Seattle, Washington, and from Vergennes, Vermont, to St. Petersburg, Florida.

In regard to the shuttle program itself, one of the key arguments against it has been that it is too expensive. Critics point out that the United States could fund a well-rounded program of unmanned spacecraft launches for about $2 billion a year. They say that most of the useful returns from space to date, such as communications, weather-observation stations in orbit, earth-surveillance data, etc., have come about through unmanned instrumented flight.

NASA has countered this by saying that it is precisely the unmanned programs of this sort that the shuttle is designed to serve. In so doing, money will be saved in launch costs and in the way spacecraft are built, deployed, serviced, and returned to earth

This view of the earth was taken from the Geostationary Operational Environmental Satellite-I (GOES-1) on October 25, 1975. Clearly visible are North and South America and the west coast of Africa.

for refurbishment and reuse. NASA believes that as much as 80 percent of the shuttle's payloads for the foreseeable future will probably consist of unmanned spacecraft.

But even so, NASA says that the achievements of the shuttle crews, both men and women, will more than pay for the additional costs required to send humans into space along with machines. As advanced as computers are, and as sophisticated as equipment has become, there still is no adequate substitute for the human being as a general sensor, calculator, evaluator, manipulator, or fixer.

One of the key disagreements between NASA and its critics has centered over how shuttle expenses are to be charged. Critics have said that the shuttle program will cost $30 to $40 billion or more to develop and operate. But NASA says these figures are wrong and so is the logic behind them. NASA believes the development costs of the shuttle should be separated, and that once the program is operational, the cost of each particular flight should be added to the cost of the mission itself. This is because much of the funding for these missions will be paid for by the users of the shuttle.

For example, if it is a Spacelab flight, the European Space Agency would reimburse NASA for the cost of launching the laboratory into orbit and returning it to earth. Or if Western Electric is putting up a new commercial communications satellite, it would pay NASA to launch it. The same would be true for missions involving the Defense Department, other government agencies and institutions, private industry, and individual research organizations, and individuals.

NASA officials say that the United States, historically, has followed such policies in the growth of its transportation systems. They point out that the railroads of the nineteenth century and the airlines of the twentieth century were both heavily subsidized by the federal government during their developmental stages. But once they became operational, each of these systems was taken over, operated, and paid for by its users. NASA believes the shuttle will lead to this same sort of evolution in space.

Thus, by not adding the estimated $20 million per flight operational cost of each mission to the total expense of the program, NASA says shuttle-development costs actually will run to less than $7.5 billion, and not to a figure three, four, or more times that amount as has been argued by critics.

Another major source of controversy between proponents and critics of the shuttle has been over actual flight costs. Critics say that the shuttle would have to be flown more often than is practical to justify its cost by comparison to the unmanned rocket-launch systems of today. NASA says this is not true, and that by using the shuttle, total space-mission expense can be reduced by more than $1 billion a year.

This argument is based on an in-depth study of projected flight requirements for a twelve-year period from 1980 through 1991. Over this period, NASA forecasts the need for 580 shuttle missions, or 48 a year. This number of flights is calculated on present-day launch rates and projected requirements for scientific, technical, military applications and for commercial cargoes.

And even this estimate may be conservative, NASA officials feel, because once the shuttle is operational and demonstrates substantial cost savings, requests for space on it will increase. This in itself could create a "productivity spiral" effect. That is, the more the shuttle is used to capacity, the less the cost to users will be; the more attractive the cost factor is, the more it will encourage additional users.

"We should not forget that America was discovered by men who were looking for spices on the other side of the world," says Dr. James C. Fletcher, former NASA administrator. "I believe we would be blind and very foolish if we do not anticipate much greater use of near-earth space when the shuttle becomes available."

Nevertheless, by applying just the 580 missions over a twelve-year period, NASA says total launch costs, including the purchase of replacement boosters, will be about $8 billion. Launch-related costs using conventional rocket systems for the 580 flights would run to just over $13 billion. So here, alone, the savings are projected to be more than $5 billion.

Payload costs for this number of flights from 1980 through 1991—again using current conventional launch systems—are estimated to be about $35 billion. But by using the shuttle, some payloads, such as satellites, could be refitted and reused. The payload cost of the 580 missions using the shuttle are estimated to be less than $27 billion. This represents savings of more than $8 billion.

So together, the launch and the payload savings that can be made by using the shuttle amount to $13 billion for the twelve-year period, or more than $1 billion a year.

The economies of shuttle use are even further accentuated by comparing actual payload costs per pound. With today's systems, it costs roughly $900 for each pound of payload rocketed into space. But because the shuttle will carry much larger loads, and it will not be necessary to build expensive backup systems and microminiaturized parts in satellites, the cost of payloads on a full shuttle flight can be reduced to about $160 a pound.

The entire cost of the shuttle's development program, NASA says, can be regained over the first few years of operation. NASA officials ask, Where else can you find such a favorable return on investment?

11

The Industrialization
of Space

No one, not even the most farsighted optimist, can yet predict how great an impact the shuttle era will have on the United States and the rest of the world for the remainder of the twentieth century and beyond. But it is becoming more apparent that this new space transportation system may well trigger a vast new industrial revolution.

The shuttle, in the 1980s and 1990s, will spur economic and industrial growth in much the same way as the railroads did in the nineteenth century and the development of aviation did during the first half of the twentieth.

More immediate benefits of such a revolution will be advanced communications systems that will enable all the earth's peoples

to know and understand each other better through virtually instantaneous communication. Also, the harnessing of solar power
and the projected establishment of huge solar and other electric
power stations in orbit, directing their almost inexhaustible
sources for use on earth, should provide a permanent solution to
the world's energy problems.

Beyond this, it is not difficult to envision

• The construction of space factories in orbit.
• The development of biological research facilities and the manufacturing of miracle drugs and vaccines in a weightless environment impossible to duplicate on earth.
• The assignment of spatial "dumps" for the harmless dispersion
of nuclear wastes and other pollutants.
• The operation of convoys of space freighters carrying lodes of
minerals and other natural resources from the moon, the asteroid
belt, and neighboring planets for harvesting on earth or in near-
earth orbiting manufacturing centers.

Such imminent possibilities are no longer the sole domain of
a few visionaries. Today the businessman and woman, as well as
the scientist, foresee the unparalleled potential of exploiting
space. In fact, many companies in the United States and in other
countries are already hard at work on practical planning to take
advantage of the coming industrial era of space created by the
shuttle.

NEW BOOM IN COMMUNICATIONS

In the communications field, for example, RCA, Western
Union, and Comsat General are three American companies that
already own complete satellite systems. IBM (International Busi-

ness Machines) also is entering this booming business. Chester Lee, NASA Space Transport System director, says, "Just to meet projected long-distance telephone requirements in the year 2000, we are going to need fifty or more satellites."

Within a few years new developments fostered by researchers at these and other firms will bring the cost of using satellite communications down to a more economical level where even small companies can employ such systems to speed business information anywhere in the world.

Currently most satellite-communications traffic is routed through satellites to large earth stations, which then transmit the messages to customers over expensive and sometimes relatively slow land lines. New systems being developed for use in the 1980s will make it possible for data to be beamed directly from satellite to more inexpensive, smaller antennas that can be erected anywhere a customer wants, even on the rooftops of company buildings.

Such "personalized," almost instantaneous service can be used in many ways. For example, when exploration ships for oil companies are searching for new sources of oil beneath the ocean floor, they generate tremendous amounts of information during seismic studies. This data has to be processed and analyzed so experts on board the ship can know whether to continue their efforts in the area already being explored. Such information, ferried by helicopter from the ship to land, takes days. But with satellite-station equipment aboard, the job could be done in hours.

By having their own ground stations linked into satellite systems, companies could annually save millions of dollars in time and travel expenses. Instead of having employees from outlying plants and field offices fly thousands of miles to a headquarters site for management meetings, seminars, or training programs, such sessions could be conducted live on closed-circuit television. Additionally, salespersons could better serve clients at distant sites in the same way.

As networks of communication satellite systems become a reality in the shuttle era, and the cost of ground transmitting and receiving stations is reduced, the range of business uses will increase. Realizing this limitless potential, a number of major corporations are today investing millions of dollars in research efforts to take advantage of this new enterprise.

The possibilities offered by having larger communications satellites carried in parts to space aboard the shuttle and assembled and deployed in orbit almost defy the imagination. One idea that is being considered is the development of a 300-foot-wide satellite. It would have the capacity to enable individuals a continent apart to communicate with each other by way of "Dick Tracy-type" receivers the size of a wristwatch. The estimated cost for such talks would be only 10 cents a minute.

The assembly of superlarge structures in orbit offers other exciting possibilities, also. One proposal calls for the deployment of a complex of mirrors nearly a square mile in diameter. By using the sun's reflected rays, up to 36,000 square miles of earth could be illuminated at night with a brightness ten times greater than that of the full moon. Such a concentration of light would have many possible applications, ranging from deterring crime on otherwise dark city streets to allowing farmers in tropical regions to work during the coolness of night.

NEW ENERGY SYSTEMS

The use of shuttle-launched satellites to ease the earth's energy problems is also under serious study. Today there is much controversy over the building of nuclear-power stations near heavily populated areas. There is fear of radiation contamination should there be an accident or leakage from such a plant. But under one concept, nuclear stations would be built in remote, sparsely settled sites, such as in deserts or between shielding mountains. Power then would be beamed, like floodlights, via microwave to a satellite's large reflectors, then relayed back to microwave receivers. Power-conversion and -distribution plants would make it available to cities without danger. A satellite reflector 2,000 feet in diameter could bounce back as much electrical energy every twenty-four hours as could be produced by nearly a quarter million barrels of oil.

Another idea being worked on by such large aerospace companies as Grumman and McDonnell Douglas calls for the establishment of large solar-energy collectors mounted on platforms in low orbit. Shuttles could service such platforms and bring the collected electrical power back to earth.

Two proposed teleoperator space spiders, seen at top left and bottom right of circular structure, build a support for a solar-power satellite onto a space-shuttle external tank. The spider would be a self-contained system with rolls or spools of coded and prestamped building materials. The shuttle orbiter is shown at top right.

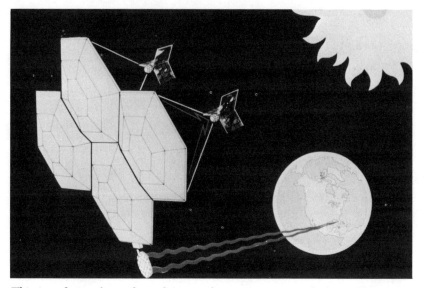

This is a design for a thermal-space solar-power station, which would generate electricity from solar heat and transmit energy to earth by way of microwave radio beam.

Other companies, like Boeing and Raytheon, are considering the practicality of building giant power-generating satellites which would directly beam solar power harnessed in space for immediate use on earth. One advanced design is for a satellite that would contain billions of solar cells on panels covering fifty square miles in space. It would be capable of delivering 10,000 megawatts to earth by microwave.

A satellite of this kind would be able to produce twice the power generated by Grand Coulee, the nation's largest hydroelectric dam. Forty-five such satellites could match the present total electrical generating power of the United States, freeing oil, coal, and their derivatives for other critical needs.

Dr. Roger W. Johnson of the Grumman Aerospace Corporation says the technology exists today to build three-by-five-mile solar-power satellites, each capable of producing 5,000 megawatts

In the neutralized gravity environment of the neutral buoyancy simulator at NASA's Marshall Space Flight Center in Alabama *(top)*, a space-suited employee joins two structural beams. This is a task that will be carried out in space after the beam builder has done its job. A beam builder *(bottom)*, utilizing the payload-bay area of a space-shuttle orbiter as its work base, fabricates the fourth and final supporting beam of a structure as a step for a proposed space solar-power station.

of power, and beaming the power to earth as microwave energy. He also predicts automated fabricating machines will be installed on space platforms that will turn out half-mile-long metal beams like giant erector-set parts, which technicians, working from the shuttle, will assemble into huge energy-gathering satellites.

"We have the engineering and the paperwork behind us," Dr. Johnson says. "We can build a space power station by 1995 if we are prepared to spend from $15 billion to $25 billion."

Of course, such projects are today economically impractical. But by the 1980s or 1990s they may not be, for some very important reasons. The shuttle will greatly reduce the cost of erecting and servicing such satellites. Present sources of energy on earth are being rapidly depleted, and as they are, their cost is rising. And the sun, inevitably, will be the earth's primary source of energy supply in the centuries to come. It is safe, pollution free, and almost inexhaustible.

MANUFACTURING IN SPACE

Before the end of this century, that is, within the next twenty years, experiments made possible by the shuttle's routine access to space will create a whole new industry—orbital manufacturing. This concept already has been proved to an extent through preliminary experiments conducted by astronauts aboard the Skylab missions of the early 1970s.

And as with communications and energy programs, leading industries in the United States and Europe, and in other areas of the world, are committing research funds toward the development of factories in earth orbit. These manufacturers and processors are interested in the high promise of in-space production of everything from semiconductors to glass to medicine.

Experiments in the weightless environment of space will result in new products impossible to make on earth. Metal foam might be one. Experts believe it will be possible to manufacture a foamed steel as light as balsa wood but with many of the properties of solid steel. Without gravity, gases formed during the processing of foamed metals would remain entrapped in the liquid metal, producing a light, spongelike material. On earth, however, gravity forces these gas bubbles to the surface so the same effect cannot be created.

Similar techniques might be used in space to mix materials so vastly different that they often cannot be combined on earth, such as steel and glass, oil and water. Glass manufacturers say ultrapure products such as high-quality lenses for lasers and optical instruments will be produced much more easily in space because impurities in production caused by the need for containers on earth will be eliminated. In gravity-free orbit, no containers will be necessary.

Metallic materials also can be easily levitated and held in place, melted and resolidified, in orbit without becoming contaminated or deformed. It is this type of processing, pretested to a degree aboard Skylab, that will produce perfect metallic spheres for use as ball bearings. This will create greater mobility and dependability for wheels and other things.

Also pretested is the growth of crystals in space, which may represent a sizable industry of the future. Such growth on earth is limited by contaminants and outside forces caused by gravity. In space, though, there would be no such limits to potential growth. Giant crystals thus could be used as very large power transistors. Pure quartz crystals could be cut into optical blanks for the production of near-perfect lenses.

Experts say factories in space will feature almost wearless machinery. Without the physical constraints of gravity, workers and equipment would move about far more easily. The individual productivity of workers would increase because of the lower amounts of energy expended. There would be few negative side effects, such as pollution, congestion, and safety hazards.

MEDICINE

The impurity-free environment of space also intrigues makers of such medical products as drugs and vaccines. The possibilities here were dramatically illustrated in 1975 aboard the Apollo-Soyuz joint American-Russian space flight. In one experiment during this mission, the rare and highly expensive enzyme urokinase was separated from human cell cultures six times more efficiently than has ever been achieved on earth.

Urokinase, which is used for the treatment of blood clotting, costs today $1,000 or more per dose. But the company officials who manufacture it believe this cost can be cut to $100 or less per dose through savings that can be made by processing it in orbit.

The separation and isolation of bacteria—difficult on earth, easy in space—and the production of vaccines without fear of contamination by impurities so prevalent on earth is a future industry being looked into by pharmaceutical companies. Much research-and-development work underway today will lead to free-flying biological-processing laboratories in orbit.

RESOURCE EXPLORATION

The shuttle may revolutionize the oil and petroleum industry, too. One way will be through high-quality surveying of the earth of much greater depth, coverage, and quality than now possible through such conventionally launched spacecraft as Landsat. Major corporations interested in earth exploration to find new supplies of natural resources, such as Exxon, Bethlehem Steel, U.S. Gypsum, and Union Oil, have even formed their own advisory organization, called Geosat Committee, Inc. Geosat is helping advise NASA on the types of services its members consider most important.

"With satellites alone, we are seeing structural geological features we could not see before," says Dr. Frederick Henderson III, the Geosat Committee's president. "We would like to have geologists aboard some of these shuttle flights because of the contributions they can make. Obviously, there is no way of knowing what the shuttle, working with improved satellites, will turn up. But if only one copper deposit or one 100-million-barrel oil field is found, the cost of one of these space systems would be more than paid for."

Another potential spin-off benefit of advanced and constant surveying from space may be the discovery of geothermal energy sources beneath the surface of the earth. Infrared and other highly sophisticated instruments may be able to detect unknown heat-generation sources that cause such natural energy-producing phenomena as geysers and volcanic flows. If these sources can be pinpointed and better understood, scientists believe they can become important future suppliers of pollution-free power.

CELESTIAL MINING

With the shuttle, the search for new and greater lodes of raw materials will not be limited to earth itself. Rich untapped fields of minerals lie waiting on the moon, on Mars and other planets, and in the asteroid belt between Mars and Jupiter. This could lead to another new and exciting industry, perhaps a major one of the twenty-first century—spatial prospecting and mining.

Even now engineers are working on designs for powerful electromagnetic engines that could dislodge asteroids from their solar orbits and push them into near-earth orbits where they could be mined whenever new mineral supplies on earth were needed.

TRANSPORTATION

Another industry on which the space shuttle undoubtedly will have immense impact is transportation. Today the Concorde jet liner can fly from Europe to the United States in a little more than four hours. But some experts believe rocket-powered craft, employing shuttle-design concepts, will be able to whisk passengers to sites halfway around the world in forty-five minutes or less.

Such vehicles would be launched vertically in suborbital trajectories aimed at a precise destination. They would reenter the atmosphere and glide unpowered to an altitude where conventional jet engines would be started to control the descent and landing on conventional runways.

With the development of the shuttle, the technology for such flights is now available. The only prohibiting factor is cost. And transportation experts point out that it takes much less energy to put an object in earth orbit than it does to fly the same object across the United States. So, they contend, there is no reason why the cost of rocket-powered flight should not become as low or lower than that of jets.

TOURISM

Few people will be able to afford the first tourist flights into space, and it may be near the end of this century before such journeys begin. But they will come, in time. Paul Siegler, president of Earth/Space, Inc., a California consulting firm contracted to NASA to study the impact of space industrialization over the next thirty years, has researched tourism possibilities.

"We're looking at people who would pay $50,000 for a few days in space," he says. "In time, that could be cut to $5,000. I see a 100-room hotel up there (in orbit) in about the year 2000, when the tourist traffic really starts to move."

These are just a few representative examples of how the shuttle will trigger a new industrial revolution in space. Some experts are now predicting that by the end of the twentieth century, business in space will have generated revenues that could reach the neighborhood of $20 billion to $30 billion. Siegler says that transmission of information, solar power, and a fledgling tourist industry —all spawned by the shuttle—will generate between $6 billion and $19 billion alone in revenues in the next two decades. Space processing of metals, glass, and medicines will add another $2 billion to $10 billion, he believes.

Experts also foresee the taking over by private enterprise of more and more areas now funded and controlled by the federal government, as the business community capitalizes on opportunities springing from industrialization. One specialist who feels that the role of business in orbit will expand greatly in the remaining years of this century is Dr. Klaus Heiss, president of Econ, Inc., a Princeton, New Jersey, firm which does a lot of research work for NASA.

"Industrial space activities, with or without financial participation by government, will develop and sustain themselves entirely, based on pursuit of economic interests," he says. "Once this point is reached, the space program will have become truly irreversible. Economic self-interest, again and again, has proven to be the most lasting historical motivation for human activity."

And yet all these projections, ambitious as they are, reveal only a fraction of what may unfold in the years ahead. Still disguised are the unexpected uses, discoveries, and dividends which history has proved often outweigh the planned payoffs.

In most instances the technology to develop and build on such enterprises is either available now or soon will be. The shuttle will make this new business frontier possible so that we may reap the munificent benefits from it well within our lifetimes.

12

Toward Cities in Orbit

In addition to stimulating a new industrial revolution, the shuttle will also be an essential factor in the eventual colonization of space. In effect, the shuttle orbiter will serve, as the Skylab served earlier, as a temporary mini-space station.

Perhaps before the end of this century, Americans will erect more permanent stations in orbit and inhabit them for periods up to six months and longer. The crew and the components for such a station will be ferried to and from orbit via the shuttle. Supplies, equipment, and replacement crew members then can be flown to the station as needed.

While the actual design and development of such a station are still in the earliest preliminary stages—and changes may occur often as we learn more about the orbital environment in the shuttle era—there are some aspects that most officials agree on today.

It is likely, for example, that the initial station or stations will be modular in construction, much like the way many school classrooms are built today. Not only is this type of configuration relatively simple to put together, but also it can be added to easily.

The station will be designed for a minimum lifetime of ten years. To remain useful for that period of time, it must be capable of evolutionary change to meet new requirements. Such flexibility is needed in any kind of laboratory, whether on earth or in orbit. As one type of activity is completed, it will be replaced by another with new support needs. New apparatus must be installed, old systems modified, and the training and makeup of the crew changed. Again modular-constructed stations would best serve these purposes.

The first station will probably provide living accommodations for a crew of twelve men and women. While the average tour of duty may be six months or a year, a shuttle could be flown to the station on short notice, perhaps in a day, in case of emergencies. Crews will consist mostly of scientists who will conduct a variety of long-term experiments in space; and applications specialists, such as geologists, hydrologists, meteorologists, and others. At least one or two members will be engineers trained to operate, maintain, and repair the station's systems.

Because the crew will be so isolated for such a long period of time—much like Antarctic expedition teams—great care will be taken in the selection of everyday living facilities. Food will be as like as possible to that served on earth. Fresh frozen meats and vegetables will be included on the menu.

While room will necessarily be tight, there will be enough

space for quiet private quarters in which individuals can work, read, write, meditate, and sleep. There will be no fancy bathroom facilities, but personal hygiene areas will be adequate enough to allow the crew members to keep themselves clean and well groomed.

The first station may weigh as much as 100,000 pounds when fully assembled, and it may have as many as five separate decks in an overall cylinder design. In one concept, two of these decks would be used for living, eating, sleeping, and controlling the "home" in space. One deck might be used to receive and store supplies. One would contain such subsystems as environmental control to maintain a pure, breathable atmosphere, and water management to reclaim waste water for reuse. And the fifth deck might be a laboratory, equipped to carry out a wide variety of experiment activities. Smaller modules, pallets or platforms, could be attached to this deck for additional experiments and equipment.

Power for operation of the station could be supplied either by a nuclear power system, or, assuming the technology has been developed by then, by large solar-cell arrays.

The crew will live in an earthlike environment, breathing in an atmosphere much like that of air at sea level. Yet they will maneuver about effortlessly—much as was done on Skylab—in the weightlessness of space. If, however, it is also advantageous to maintain gravity conditions similar to those on earth, this can be done by swinging the station in circles, counterbalanced by a discarded space booster tank connected to the station.

Much of the work done today by satellites, and to be continued in the 1980s during the shuttle era, will be greatly advanced and expanded on permanent stations in orbit. In science, new technological breakthroughs will be forged in the fields of oceanography,

Activity at a manned, modularized space station in earth orbit. The modules, at right center, house laboratory equipment and provide working and living space for the crew members of the space station. Above the modular configuration, a space solar-power station is under construction. An orbiter is at upper left.

meteorology, biology, medicine and the life sciences, astronomy, physics, and chemistry. Earth services will include improved communications, education, and transportation systems, more accurate long-range weather forecasts and storm-warning systems, and round-the-clock surveillance of agricultural, mineral, petroleum, and other resources.

Orbiting factories, medical processing and manufacturing centers and hospitals, and solar-power complexes will be managed and operated by station crew members. Manned launches to the moon and the asteroid belt to mine raw-material supplies will become routine. More distant manned flights to Mars and other planets may originate at or near the station. Crew members will assemble the rockets and service the spacecraft in orbit. Small groups of settlers will colonize the moon and use it as a supply base.

Giant antennas will be erected near the station and be tuned to the universe to search for signs of other intelligent life, somewhere in our galaxy of stars or beyond, which probably will be initially picked up in the form of radio signals.

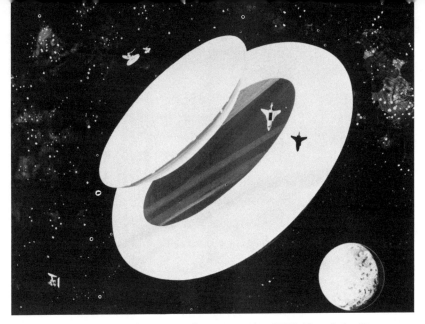

Giant antennas, such as this intermediate-size space SETI (Search for Extraterrestrial Intelligence) system, will be erected near space stations.

As humans adapt to their new environment on a more permanent basis, the mini-colony will grow in size, perhaps through the addition of clusters of stations. Then larger, completely self-sustaining bases will be built in space. Full-scale settlements of people will live and work in orbit for long periods of time, eventually for lifetimes. One popular concept that has been proposed and is under study has three principal stages. The first would be a small-scale model community that some experts say could be achieved in this century. The main base would be a sphere about a mile in circumference, housing a population of some ten thousand.

Next would come a medium-size settlement with an outside chance of realization by the year 2000. But more likely, it would come later, in the first part of the twenty-first century. It would involve a cylinder 4 miles in diameter and 20 miles long, with five hundred square miles of living space and a population of several million.

Beyond this would be larger settlements, 15 miles in diameter and 75 miles long, containing seven thousand square miles of useful space and more millions of humans. Life on these "spatial cities" would be much like that on earth. The inhabitants would have gravity, air, land, water, and natural sunshine. But they would be free of pollution and such natural disasters as hurricanes, tornadoes, volcanoes, tidal waves, and blizzards. Temperature, atmosphere, and weather would be climate-controlled.

High-yield agriculture and high-quality industry could provide ample food and full employment for all inhabitants. Additionally, people could enter weightless rooms or dynariums through air locks to participate in three-dimensional recreational activities.

If all of this sounds like fantasy or science fiction, consider that just a generation ago the manned exploration of the moon and spacecraft expeditions to distant planets were believed to be equally preposterous.

The fact is that all the technology to carry out these endeavors is either available today or soon will be. The shuttle will be a fully operational orbital transportation system in the 1980s. Space stations could be erected and manned well before the end of this century. And permanent space colonies and even advanced civilizations are definitely conceivable within our lifetime.

The question then is not if or how. It is when. Technology will not be the limiting factor. The United States proved this through the Apollo program of the 1960s by placing astronauts on the moon and returning them safely to earth only eight years after the lunar landing had been declared a national goal of high ranking.

How soon we colonize space and use its endless potential for the betterment of all mankind will be a matter of national and international priorities. The more funds and resources we devote to such a project, the faster we will accomplish it.

Already, thousands of people in this country and in others around the world are coming to the realization that the only long-term alternative to an earth chaotically short of food, land, and natural resources, and with its air and water polluted beyond saving, is through the establishment of life in the ultimate frontier—space.

By building our power stations and our factories and by mining resources in space, earth can be maintained as the ecological garden spot of the solar system. Earth's unique features—its rich soil, its teeming oceans, its life-sustaining bioatmosphere, can thus be preserved and protected for centuries to come.

Even so, the industrial colonization of space offers many things that earth cannot for future generations. It offers unlimited reserves of raw materials and unlimited low-cost energy sources. It offers a new opportunity for international cooperation and understanding among all nations and peoples striving for a common goal. It offers a higher quality of life for all humanity and the potential to eliminate forever such earthly afflictions as poverty, hunger, disease, and illiteracy.

Perhaps even more important, it offers new challenges and fresh opportunities for a progress-oriented earth civilization that has exhausted terrestrial frontiers. The human race as we know it today will cease to develop and be forever condemned to solitary confinement on one small planet only if these challenges and opportunities go unheeded.

Space orbiters and other celestial bodies are the new frontiers of our time. The space shuttles of the 1980s will be the historical but modest first steps on a journey that knows no end.

Index

Henderson, Frederick, 101
Holmes, Oliver Wendell, 16
Houston Control Center, 9
hypersonic flight range, 26

Inertial Upper Stage (IUS), 58–59, 72
Intelsat satellites, *75*
intercontinental ballistic missiles (ICBMs), 69
International Business Machines (IBM), 92–93
international space programs, 53, 60–66
Isabella of Spain, Queen, 84

jet pilots, 38–39, 43, 47
Johnson, Roger W., 96–98
Johnson Space Center, 7, 45
Jupiter, 58

Kennedy Space Center, 1–4, *5*, 7, *11*, 15, *32*, 48, 54, 56–57
Kerwin, Joseph, 20–21, 56
Kraft, Christopher, 45

Landsat earth-resource surveillance program, 57, 60–61, 77, *79*, 100
land-use information, 21, 76–78, 100–101
Lee, Chester, 93
life, extraterrestrial, 109
liquid propellants, 4, 30–31
Long Duration Exposure Facility (LDEF), 52–54
    cost of experiments on, 55
    "Getaway Special" experiments on, 54–56
Lousma, Jack, 21, 24
Lucid, Shannon W., *45*
lunar landings, manned, 12–14, 39, 40–41, 61, 68, 85, 110
lunar studies, LDEF, 53

Mariner flights, 58
Marshall Space Flight Center, 36–37, *97*
Mars space flights, 68, 108

material processing, 65
mechanical wear, 99–100
medical experiments, 9, 21, 64–65, 100
medical technology, 81, 100
Mercury Project, 38, 39, 40
Mercury spacecraft, 17–18, 43
metal alloys, 24, 65, 99
metal foam, 99
meteoroid particles, 53–54
meteorological data, 14, 61, 69, 71, 76
Michoud Assembly Facility, *31*
micrometeoroid-detection panels, 53–54
microwave-communications gear, 48
microwave power reflectors, 95
military attacks, surprise, 69
military satellites, 57, 67–72
miniaturized equipment, 51, 90
mining, extraterrestrial, 92, 101–102
minority groups, astronauts from, 45
mission simulators, 47
mission specialists, 43–44, 45, 46
mitt, pneumatically operated, *81*
Mondale, Walter, 85
moon:
    colonies on, 108
    landings on, 12–14, 39, 40, 61, 68, 85, 110
    Taurus Littrow area of, 40
    volcanic activity on, 40
moon-rocket launches, 4
Multi-Mode lights, *83*

National Aeronautics and Space Administration (NASA), 2, 12–13, 15, 26, 32, 48, *66*, 74, 76, 79, 102–103
    arguments for space program of, 86–90
    astronaut requirements of, 38–46
    Dryden Flight Research Center of, 33–36
    employees of, 86–87
    international programs and, 60–66
    Skylab program of, 17–24, 55, 56, 105
    space experiments of, 53–55

ABOUT THE AUTHOR

L. B. Taylor, Jr., has worked in and around the space industry at Cape Canaveral and the Kennedy Space Center during most of the major manned and unmanned launches. He is the author or coauthor of four previous books on aerospace subjects, and also of a number of others having buried treasure, careers in chemistry, and teen-age heroes and heroines as their subjects. In addition, he has had more than 225 articles published in major national magazines.

An avid traveler, Mr. Taylor makes his home in Williamsburg, Virginia, with his wife and three children.